D1177212

OUTRAGEOUSLY ORGANIZED

Ten Professional Organizers Share Their Trade Secrets

By

SUZETTE GAVIN
ELLEN HANKES
ASHLEY KATES
JAN LIMPACH
SHERI LUKASIEWICZ
CYNDY SALZMANN
DONNA SCHOEPPNER
DIANE SULLIVAN
AMY TOKOS
TRACI WATKINS

Outrageously Organized © 2012 by Suzette Gavin, Ellen Hankes, Ashley Kates, Jan Limpach , Sheri Lukasiewicz , Cyndy Salzmann, Donna Schoeppner, Diane Sullivan, Amy Tokos and Traci Watkins

All rights reserved, including the right to reproduce this book or portions thereof in any form whatsoever. For information, contact: Diane Sullivan, 402-253-8145, diane@organization-station.net

10 9 8 7 6 5 4 3 2 1

Printed by CreateSpace,
a division of Amazon, Inc.,Charleston, SC 29418
CreateSpace is a registered trademark of Amazon, Inc.

Manufactured in the United States of America

For information regarding special discounts for bulk purchases, please contact: Diane Sullivan, 402-253-8145, diane@organization-station.net.

Library of Congress Cataloging-in-Publication Data LCCN 2010912961
CreateSpace, North Charleston, SC

ISBN-10: 1453789308
EAN-13: 9781453789308

www.outrageouslyorganized.com

Contents

Introduction

We all know her. And secretly hate her.

She's the mom from the baseball team who never forgets it's her turn for treats. She invites you to "stop by anytime"—and means it. And she always looks put together—even when driving carpool.

How *does* she do it? What's her secret?

You may have even asked her how she stays so organized—and she likely demurred with a sly "Oh, I'm really not *that* organized..."

Today—she's busted. Exposed. Outed.

For the first time, ten organizing professionals dish about the secrets of the trade. Taking questions from princesses of procrastination from Seattle to Syracuse, they have put together the ultimate 4-1-1 on getting—and staying—organized.

- Amy, your family management expert, will share ideas and inspiration for making the most of family time and keeping rug rats from spoiling the rug.

- Ashley will give you the knowhow to maintain a method for eliminating the chaos.

- Cyndy, affectionately known as America's Clutter Coach, will help you develop the expertise to sift trash form treasure.

- Diane is a virtuoso of timesaving techniques that will help you find time to have *fun*.

- Donna is the simplicity specialist.

- Ellen helps chronically disorganized people put the clamp on clutter.

- Jan, your Oracle of Organization, enjoys helping people find what they need, when they need it.

- Sheri brings peace to your life and spaces.

- Suzette is a creative problem solver whose inventive skills and talents work when you think they won't.

- Traci is your organizer of hopes, dreams, and stray paperwork. She'll change your world with her organizing skills and positive outlook.

By the way, there's no need to worry that these organizing professionals will tell her they've spilled their trade secrets. She'll just think you're *outrageously organized*.

Ellen Hankes, CPO-CD©

Finding Balance

Our family should be pictured next to the definition of "crazy busy." I'd like to simplify but have no idea where to start.

—Mom on the Go

Periodically the tires on my car need balancing. I let the experts at the tire center take care of redistributing the weights on each tire to accommodate the wear that occurs over time. The result is better mileage, a more comfortable ride, and increased life of the tires.

Periodically, our lives need rebalancing so we are able to get more done, enjoy life to the fullest, and become healthier. An honest assessment of the amount of time we spend at work, with our families, taking care of our own needs, and helping others is often the place to begin.

Here's a short quiz to see if your life needs to be rebalanced:

- Is there a difference between your work days and your weekends?

- Do you schedule time for yourself?

- Do you take at least one planned vacation (or stay-cation) each year?

- Have you helped someone in the past week?

- Is there something (event, social gathering, project, etc.) you're looking forward to in the near future?

If you answered "Yes" to three or more of these questions, you likely lead a balanced life. Only one or two "Yes" answers may indicate you have an opportunity to improve the balance in your life.

You may be thinking, "That's easy for you to say." Well, it's actually easier than you may imagine. Here's how to get started:

1. Sit down with your family and make a list of your priorities.

2. Compare your schedule to your priorities. How do they match up?

3. If you're spending your time and energy on things that aren't important to you, make adjustments.

Making those adjustments is often the most difficult part for people. Small things such as scheduling family time or delegating responsibilities can make a big difference. Just like a well-balanced car, a balanced life makes it much easier to stay on course.

Ellen

Diane
Sullivan

D Is for Declutter

I know I need to get organized but have no idea where to start. Any advice?

—Wondering in Wahoo

The organizing process is not as hard as you may think. It all begins with decluttering. Here's how to get started: Pick one room to work on. A lot of people choose the bedroom because that's where they begin their day. The idea is to remove things that don't fit your vision for the space. Bring in five containers labeled "Donate," "Designate," "Dough," "Decide later," and "Discard."

- **Donate.** By donating an item you no longer use to a thrift store, it gets a new lease on life. For example, you may have a nice suit hanging in your closet that doesn't fit. That suit could have a new life when worn by a jobless woman going for an interview or a mom attending her daughter's wedding.

- **Designate.** This box is for items you would like to pass on to specific people. It may be something you borrowed or an item you would like to give to family or friends. For example, you may offer the novel on your nightstand to your sister-in-law—or finally get around to returning the bracelet you borrowed from your neighbor. People get their stuff, and you get back your space.

- **Dough.** Some things have a lot of monetary value, so I'm not suggesting that you just give everything away. It's important to be realistic, and selling your items is another way to downsize your belongings. The Internet can be a great tool for making some extra money if you do your research and don't procrastinate. Another option is to have a garage sale. But remember, this takes a lot of time and energy to get ready and run for two or three days. Only you can decide if your time is worth the effort.

- **Decide later.** Items you're not ready to part with belong in this box. Maybe you have clothes that don't fit, but you're not ready to give them away. Close this box, date it, and put it away. If after a year there are items in the box you haven't used, your decision has been made. You don't need them.

- **Discard.** This box is for items that no one else can use—a.k.a. *junk*. Put these items promptly in the trash or recycle bin.

This five-box method can be used to tackle a whole room whether you have five days, five hours, or just five minutes.

Diane

Jan
Limpach

Organizing 101

My life is so disorganized. I need help with day-to-day stuff. What do you suggest?

—Looking for Order

Organization is key to having smooth, stress-free days. A good way to start is to get the organizing basics mastered and then fine-tune as you go. Here are some principles that will serve as the foundation for order and organization in your living or work space:

Put like with like. Imagine walking into a grocery store where one can of beans is on a shelf next to the cinnamon, and the bananas are in the freezer section with the ice cream. It's so much easier to shop when like items are with each other. It just makes more sense when the beans are with the canned vegetables and bananas are with the fresh fruit. In the same way, your house will make more sense when you put like things together. Gather all the magazines in one spot. Find all the games and put them together.

Everything has a home. Think about the silverware drawer, where there are spaces for spoons, knives, and forks. It's easy to put away the silverware because each piece has a spot. Your mail or batteries, for example, may not have defined places like this, so your task is to define a home for each kind of item. Of course, the fewer items you have, the fewer homes you need for them. A well-defined space known to all family members will make it easier for things to be found and, hopefully, put away.

Set aside time to organize each day. It will help if you aren't interrupted during this period. Find a time that is most productive for you. Organizing just a little bit every day makes it easier to stay on top of the clutter. Some people like to choose one room a day and others like to focus daily on their hot-spot, such as the kitchen counter.

Personalize the process. What works well for one person may not be the answer for another. Do things that work naturally for you. Laundry is a great example of how we do our chores in different ways—a load a day or five loads once a week. Trust your instincts and do what fits your schedule. One solution does not fit everybody. Otherwise, we would all be wearing size six red pumps seven days a week.

Organization is a day-to-day affair. Master the principles by starting in the area of your home where you spend the most time. After implementing these four principles in one area, you'll have the knowhow and confidence to move on to another area.

Jan

Cyndy
Salzmann

Ten Steps to an Organized Kid

My kids create clutter in their sleep! How I can get them to be more organized?

—*Not So Keen on Clutter*

One of my favorite proverbs says, "Train a child up in the way he should go, and when he is old he will not depart from it." Here are ten tips to help kids get—and stay—organized:

1. Teach your children that less is more. The less stuff you have, the easier it is to keep things organized.

2. Avoid creating a future packrat. When it comes to your children's personal space, let them

decide what stays and what goes. It's okay if they are willing to let go of only a few things at first. Be a good role model by maintaining a clutter-free home.

3. Help kids find a "home" for everything that is easily accessible. Put bins on low shelves for toys and other possessions. Give them a special box for treasures. Install hooks at their eye level. The easier it is for children to put something away, the more likely they will do so.

4. Provide different containers for different items so kids know where to put things away without having to make a decision. I learned this lesson the hard way when my children would clean up their rooms by shoving everything under the bed.

5. Let your children help label containers and they will be more likely to use them. Allow them to be as creative as they want with the labels, either with writing or drawing pictures. Have fun with it, and your children will be more open to making the system work.

6. Make it easy to keep clothes neat. Purge closets and drawers so kids can put away their clothes without trying to squeeze them in the space. Put shoe boxes or other containers without lids in drawers to organize socks, underwear, and oth-

er smaller items. Put a large tub, box or basket in the closet for shoes.

7. Put a clothes hamper or laundry basket in each child's room. A laundry basket can collect dirty clothes in the bedroom, be brought to the laundry room, and be returned to the bedroom with clean, folded clothes. This will make it easier for kids to care for their own wardrobe.

8. Gifts don't have to take up space. Encourage relatives to give gifts that are consumable such as movie tickets, a zoo pass, or gift certificates to a favorite restaurant.

9. When your child receives a new toy or stuffed animal, encourage him or her to give one of the old toys to charity. Make this easy by placing a family donation container in a permanent spot in the house.

10. Don't forget to celebrate. When family members work together to get organized, reward them with a special treat or family outing.

It's never too soon to start teaching children sound organizing techniques. The sooner they start, the easier they learn.

Cyndy

Ashley
Kates

Once and Done Lists

I travel a lot. It amazes me that, even when I make a list, I seem to forget something. Help!

—*Always Up in the Air*

Lists are a great tool to keep us organized. Grocery lists, travel lists, babysitter lists, medication lists—and the list goes on and on.

How many of those lists do you re-create time and time again? There is a way to cut back on some of the list making and having to rethink all the items each time. Here's how:

1. Determine the kinds of lists you use repeatedly for different purposes, and save these lists on your computer. These will become your master lists.

2. For each master list, detail the things to include. For example, a travel master list would include everything you need for most trips, such as toothpaste, slippers, and medication.

3. Test-drive your master list to see if it meets your needs. Make necessary adjustments.

You now have created a standard form customized to your needs, which you can use time and time again. You can print out your master list each time you need it. If you laminate it, you can use a dry-erase marker to check off things and add items specific to the activity. A quick swipe, and it will be ready for the next time.

Lists are great time-saving tools, and master lists take it a step further. Create the list once and, you're done.

Ashley

**Sheri
Lukasiewicz**

Repurpose on Purpose

I love to be creative. One time I repurposed an old wooden kitchen chair into a planter. What are some other fun repurposing ideas?

—Resourceful

When you have a need and you're able to fill that need by using something you already possess, it gives you such a feeling of accomplishment. I get excited about repurposing, which simply means taking an item and using it in a way other than originally intended.

Some repurposing ideas can be simple to pull off, while some require a bit of revamping. I'll share a bigger repurposing project as well as some less complicated ones.

My biggest repurpose project came when we were expecting our first baby. I had quite an attraction to antique Hoosier kitchen cabinets. I found one at an antique shop near our home. My husband agreed that I could get it if I had a place and a purpose for it in our small farmhouse. Since we didn't have any baby furniture, I got the idea to turn the cabinet into a changing table. I covered the pull-out kneading table with batting, fabric, and heavy plastic. It was perfect for changing baby. All the cabinet cubbies were perfect for diapers, lotions, wipes, and baby clothes. I got many great comments on my all-in-one baby center.

That was a major repurpose task. However, there are smaller projects that might give you inspiration. My daughter-in-law's friend is quite at home with a sewing machine. She took a bunch of old neckties and made a wonderful shoulder bag for my daughter-in-law. Oh, how she treasures that purse!

When my daughter and her husband were expecting their first baby, a friend of theirs took some of his old military camo shirts and made them into a fabulous diaper bag for them.

Repurposing projects are limited only by your imagination.

Sheri

Donna
Schoeppner

What's Your Clutter Costing You?

*I'm drowning in clutter but don't have
motivation to dig out. Any suggestions to get
me moving?*

—Baffled in the Bluffs

I recommend you first think about the ways in which clutter is really costing you. It might just be the motivation that you need to get started. Clutter costs money, time, and peace of mind.

Money. Clutter can cost you money in ways that can add up quickly. Some examples include misplaced gift cards, late fees on bills and buying something you already own because you can't find it. Some people even accumulate so many things that they have to rent storage units with monthly fees. How is your clutter affecting your financial situation?

Time. Before buying something, remember that it isn't just the dollar amount of the item that must be considered. Once at your home, you then have to store it, clean it and repair it. How is your clutter affecting your time?

Peace of mind. Clutter also has an emotional cost and often increases your stress level. How do you feel when you walk into your home and you're confronted with clutter? Your home should be a welcoming and relaxing place instead of a reminder of uncompleted tasks. Clutter drains your energy and clutters your mind. How is your clutter affecting your peace of mind?

Getting organized is a process that takes time. Getting into the habit of decluttering for fifteen minutes each day goes a long way in helping organize and maintain your home. In the end, you'll be rewarded by having more money, time and peace of mind.

Donna

Traci
Watkins

Functional Filing

I work from home, and I'm having a hard time keeping my home and work papers organized. It's time for some help.

—Snowed Under

Whether your desk is the dining-room table or is in a dedicated location, setting up a paper filing system is crucial to your success. Since you work from home, it's important to separate business from personal papers. A quick start would be to sort your personal files into the following categories:

- **Financial**—tax related papers, bank statements, investments, home contracts, insurance and bills—basically anything to do with money

- **Household items**—manuals, home projects, improvement ideas, etc.

- **Family items**—birth certificates, marriage license, and other important documents

- **Reference materials**—address list, schedules, school information, and medical information

As needed, break down each category into further categories that will help you to find items faster. For example, you may want a document file for each family member. While this is a listing of personal files, you can do the same type of sorting with your business files. The categories may be different, but you get the idea.

Consider using a colored filing system (green for financial, brown for home, blue for business, red for medical, etc.). Some people like to do this, but others find this hard to maintain. Do what works best for you.

A filing system can be helpful in keeping papers under control and maintenance to a minimum. Keep the system simple to maximize your results.

Traci

Suzette
Gavin

Label Logic

*I just finished organizing my storage room.
Everything is in containers that are lined up like
soldiers—but now I can't find a thing.*

—Miss Placed Possessions

Organization needs labels like a soldier needs a dog
tag. Where would we be in a world without labels on
containers? But all labels are not created equal. Some
labels are more useful than others.

Every soldier wears a dog tag (label), and so
should your containers. Create labels large enough
so you can easily see them. Be sure they are detailed
enough so you can understand what the container
really contains. For example, when storing clothing,
label each container by season and size. You might
even break down the categories further so you know

exactly what you have in each container, for example, "Tops—Winter—Size 10."

Labels need to be on at least two locations on the container. Good places include the side and end. Ideally, when labeling tubs, a third label should be placed on top. The label on the top helps to keep the correct lid with the correct container.

Labels must be legible. Otherwise, the belts get mixed up with the boots. A label maker can be an organized girl's best friend.

Suzette

Amy
Tokos

Help! My Photos Are Stuck on My Computer

*I love scrapbooking, but I'm always behind.
The photos never make it to the scrapbook.
Help!*

—No Time for Embellishments

Scrapbooks are creative, fun, and a great way to preserve your photos. But scrapbooking stressed me out. I always felt like I was behind in maintaining the memories in an album. My scrapbooking took over a large space in the basement, and all that stuff was a huge organizing challenge. Then one of my friends showed me a photo book she had made, and I could finally see a light at the end of my scrapbooking tunnel.

I wanted my photos in a fun and organized book with captions to supplement the visual memories.

I discovered that I could go online to a user-friendly website that turns all my digital photos into a beautiful album. These personalized albums are called photo books.

When you visit a website that makes photo books, you pick out the type of album you want to make. They have lots of options on the size, cover, and page backgrounds. Make all your choices, and then download your pictures to the site. No worries—the pictures will stay on your computer as well. You can then drag your pictures to the pages of the book. It will take a few hours to make a book, but you won't have to order any prints or buy any scrapbooking gear. A computer is all that's needed. When your book is complete, you'll receive in the mail a nicely bound book containing all your pictures and memories.

If you love to scrapbook, then keep it up. Otherwise, give photo books a try. It will simplify your life.

Amy

Ellen
Hankes,
CPO-CD©

What Is Later Thinking?

Late and Later. That's my new nickname. How can I change this?

—Forever Tardy

"Ask me *later*."

"Buy now, pay *later*."

"I will do it *later*."

Later may be a simple word—just five small letters—but it carries a huge impact. Procrastinators simply love the word *later*. Chronically disorganized people often plan to get organized later. And "I'll do it later" is a phrase that often frustrates parents of teenagers.

While some people are habitually late, others are expert at coming up with delay tactics to put off something they don't feel is interesting or challenging. Independent workers with unstructured time sometimes put off until later the tasks that are of little interest or for which they lack everything they need to begin.

An inaccurate perception of time is often a challenge for those who delay tasks or projects until later. For example, it's difficult to begin a task later when you don't define what *later* means. *Later* can be later in the morning, later in the day, or just later.

Later can mean missed opportunities, feelings of failure, or disappointment. If you want to change your *later* thinking, here are several tips you can apply sooner rather than later:

- **Listen to yourself.** When you think or say later, ask yourself, "When?" Just call it later surgery.

- **Work with an accountability partner.** Ask a friend or colleague to help to you incorporate your goals into your schedule—and to hold you accountable.

- **Take a realistic look at your time.** Overcommitment can lead to postponing important work or life events.

Listen for *later* in your life. You'll be more accountable to yourself and to others. Your productivity will soar, and you'll have more time to do things that make your heart sing.

Ellen

Cyndy
Salzmann

Tiny Timesavers

I need more hours in my day! Do you have any time-saving hints—or should I just get a body double?

—Oracle of Overcommitment

First, my dear, be gentle with yourself. I suspect you're accomplishing more than you think. But I also know in today's "crazy busy" world, saving time can be found in the little things.

Here's an example. I used to stumble down to the kitchen in the morning, turn on the coffee, and stare at it while it brewed. It took more than a few mornings to realize I could be using those few minutes in a more productive way.

So now, after turning on the coffee, my morning routine is to toss a load of laundry in the washing machine, empty the dishwasher, and take dinner out of the freezer. Believe it or not—the coffee brews just fine without me watching it drip into the pot.

And, like Ellen's example of the moss rose later in this book, I've made it my habit before going upstairs to bed, to pick up the clutter in the family room, check the calendar for the next day's activities, start the dishwasher, and carry up my clean laundry to put away. This is a much better use of my time than my old habit of leaving the dishes until morning and tripping over my shoes on the way up the stairs.

Cyndy

Diane
Sullivan

Manage Those Manuals

My dishwasher recently flooded the kitchen floor. In my panic, I could not find the manual. I finally found it the next day, just a little too late. You're an organizer, so what do organizers do with their manuals?

—Troubleshooting from the Hip

A flood on the kitchen floor is cause for panic. Those product manuals usually have troubleshooting lists that are helpful in an emergency. Every household has numerous manuals: washer/dryer, electronic devices, lawn mower. Don't throw out the paperwork with the packing material. Keep the receipt and warranty information, and staple them into the manual.

There are a couple of systems you might want to consider that organizers like to use for storing these manuals. The first is to gather your manuals and place them in a central location like a drawer or a file cabinet. A drawer works well for a few manuals, and the one for your latest purchase or the one you refer to most often will always be on top. This is a quick and easy system.

If you have lots of manuals, a filing system could help you keep track of them. File the manuals in alphabetical order by what you call them. Is it a TV, a television, or an electronic item? Just label the file using the first word that comes to mind. Now, the next time the dishwasher floods the kitchen floor, you'll be able to find the manual quickly.

The next system that organizers like to share is placing manuals near the point of use. For example, this may mean storing the oven manual close to the oven for quick reference when you need to use the self-cleaning function. This system works because the lawn mower manual is always in the garage and the kitchen appliance manuals are always in the kitchen.

These two systems can stand alone, or you may want to use a combination of them. Occasionally look through your manuals and remove the ones for items you no longer own. If a manual goes missing, you can almost always find it online. Finding that manual may mean money saved due to fewer service calls.

Diane

Ashley
Kates

Don't Be Lost If You Lose Your Wallet

I've heard that I need to have a list of the items I carry in my wallet in case it gets lost or stolen. Where should I start?

—Billie Fold

Losing your wallet or having it stolen can be very scary. I hope you never have this experience, but it could happen. Organizing all the information in your wallet will help minimize the loss.

- Create a list of every important item in your wallet.

- Make copies of all credit cards, including their numbers, expirations dates, and the 800 number on the back.

- Also make copies of all the other important items in your wallet, such as your driver's license, insurance cards, and loyalty cards.

- If you carry checks, list the bank account numbers: checking and savings and any other important numbers or codes that need to be tracked.

Store your information in a safe place. Be sure to label the file something other than "Financial" or "Sensitive Information." If you file your information on a computer, don't forget to back it up and protect it with a password.

If for some reason, you lost or had your information stolen, following the list above will help speed up your recovery. You'll have a quick reference of contacts and account numbers. And you won't have to waste time gathering information on what was in your wallet.

Ashley

Sheri
Lukasiewicz

Winning the Battle of the Bulging Purse

I'm really good about being organized at home and at work, but my purse is a mess. Can you help me spend less time digging for the stuff I need?

—Handbag Hangover

First, prepare for battle. You might be surprised what is lurking in the bottom of your purse. Hidden in the darkness you might come across lint-laden cough drops or maybe worse—a couple of stiff tissues.

Here's your battle plan:

1. Empty your purse on a hand towel (or a bath towel if you need it). This will help keep small

items like earrings from rolling and dropping out of sight. It also keeps dust, lint, and crumbs from getting on your table, floor, or carpet. When you're finished, simply toss the towel into the laundry.

2. Deal with enemy combatants right away. File the receipts. Toss the crumbled crackers. You know the drill.

3. Next, go through your wallet. Dispose of expired cards and coupons. Empty out the bulk of your loose change. Look for ways to lighten your load.

4. Wipe your purse out with a damp cloth. Then take time to consider whether it's working for you. Is it too big? Too small? Too few pockets? Too many pockets? Or is it just right?

5. Finally, return *only* those items you really need.

I often recommend a purse organizer. They come in many styles and sizes that make swapping purses a snap.

With a clean and organized purse in hand, you've won the Battle of the Bulging Purse.

Sheri

Donna
Schoeppner

On-the-Go Info

When running errands, I never know the right size of household items or who needs a birthday card this week. I always have to go back to the store. Any advice?

—Running in Circles

From printer ink cartridges to Grandpa's birthday, we need to remember so many things when we shop. Take a few minutes to jot down two key lists. You will not only save yourself time, but also the frustration of having to make multiple trips.

First, keep a list of measurements, sizes and details of replacement items for your home in your wallet. That list of furnace and water-filter types, sizes of light bulbs and room measurements can save you tons of frustration when you go shopping. Your handy list will remind you that your furnace filter size is 20x25x1 (or whatever size your furnace requires). This necessary information will get you in and out of the store in no time, with exactly what you need.

Second, make a list of all the greeting cards you need for the year, and keep it in your wallet. As you find a card for each person or celebration, cross it off the list. This will prevent buying duplicate cards and result in fewer trips to the store. Prepare for unexpected life events by keeping a few sympathy or get well cards on hand. Once at home, keep all the cards in one place, so you always know where to find them.

Your on-the-go info will be your new best friend.

Donna

Traci
Watkins

The Heart of an Organized Home

I used to love to cook, but now I get frustrated before I even open the cookbook. Help!

—Cooked Goose

We've all heard the saying "The kitchen is the heart of the home." Unfortunately, when a kitchen is a disorderly mess, the only thing flowing from it is frustration.

I'm big on creating a vision and then using affirmations to help turn the vision into reality. For example, start by thinking about what you would like your kitchen to look like by finishing the statement "My organized kitchen will be..." You might complete the sentence with something like "a happy place," "a place for the family to spend time," or "a fun place to bake."

Now clear your mind of clutter by replacing negative thoughts, such as *I can barely keep up with dishes, much less get my kitchen organized,* with positive ones like *I think it would help to have a family schedule for washing the dishes.*

Finally, follow up your hard work with affirmations, such as "I love to bake in my organized kitchen" or "I love hearing about the kids' day at the dinner table."

Identifying your vision is the first step in the recipe for success.

Traci

Jan
Limpach

Magazine Issues

I have tons of magazines and catalogs. They are here, there, and everywhere. I love them but I just don't know how to store them. What's the solution?

—National Subscriber

Magazines have been arriving in households for nearly three hundred years. They are timely, entertaining, informative, and quick to read. The pictures take us into beautiful homes and promise us flawless skin. Some magazines have silky-smooth, thick pages. What's not to like about magazines and catalogs?

The challenge is to find ways to store them. Some people allocate shelving for a specified number of issues, such as the last twelve months. Magazine boxes that are open on one side and the top help floppy magazines to stand upright. Covered totes protect treasured issues from damage but make retrieving certain ones inconvenient. A coffee table or end table with closed door storage could accommodate magazines. Just make sure there is a reason you keep each magazine. Do a reality check on why the magazine is important to keep.

Magazines are guests that might be overstaying their welcome. After all, styles change. Color palettes vary. The benefit of magazines is to bring us new and updated information. New magazines come in to replace the old ones. But where do old magazines go?

Here are a few options for dealing with excess magazines and catalogs:

- Keep special recipes or craft ideas by tearing out the page and setting it aside. Put them in labeled folders or a notebook. But remember that just about any recipe or craft inspiration can be found on the Internet, so you may not need to go to the trouble of keeping the magazine version, storing it, and remembering where it is when you need it.

- Cancel the magazines and catalogs you no longer read or enjoy. Look for information inside them or on the Internet for instructions on terminating subscriptions. It's a good idea to carefully read and understand the terms of magazine subscriptions, because it can be difficult to cancel them. There are services that can assist you with this process. Just do an Internet search for "magazine cancelation" to find these services.

- Recycle magazines by passing them on to someone else. Consider hospital or doctor's reception area, nursing homes or friends. Specialty magazines such as quilting issues can be shared with others who have the same interests. School speech teams may be interested in magazine with information on timely topics. Just remember to remove personal information from the magazine or catalog before you donate it.

- Passing on magazines may take more time than you have. You may just want to throw them in your recycle bin at home. That's much quicker and easier.

Make sure the magazines you have are the ones you read and truly love. Don't clutter your space with issues you don't have the time or desire to read. Perhaps an electronic version of a magazine subscription would solve the clutter and storage problems for you. Think twice before you renew a subscription or get a new magazine. Happy reading!

Jan

Amy
Tokos

Should I Save All My Kids' Artwork?

*My kids bring home some creative artwork.
I know I can't keep every piece, but what
should I keep?*

—Picasso's Mom

As moms, we love to save mementos of our children's stages of life, especially their artwork and other expressions of their creativity. It's what we're supposed to do, right? What do you do with the zillion papers with the crusted paint? Will you pass it on to your children when they are grown up, make a huge scrapbook, or just hang on to it for your lifetime?

Recently a friend pulled me aside and told me a funny story about her adult daughter's visit over the holidays. My friend had identified a few boxes in her storage area that contained her daughter's school-work. This mom lovingly presented the storage boxes filled with school papers to her daughter. Not appreciating the collection, her daughter looked at just a few of the papers, made a few snide comments, and put all of the papers in the recycle bin.

I share this story because with four school-age children, I'm in the stage of collecting schoolwork. I'm doing this in an easy and organized manner, but my friend really gave me something to think about. Now I ask, "Why am I doing this?" The answer used to be "for my kids to have someday." And as a mom, isn't that what I'm supposed to do?

The reality is that I think my kids, like my friend's daughter, aren't going to want the stuff. They will think I'm crazy for keeping it and even crazier for giving it to them. I have a new goal: I only keep the items that I want to keep for me. It's now a small collection of items that touches my heart.

Keeping it simple. You've got to love that.

Amy

Suzette
Gavin

Store, Divide, and Conquer

Our organizing "bug" is often spontaneous, and we don't always have time to get organizing supplies. Do you have some ideas for using what we already have here at home?

—*The Queen of Quick*

A few minutes here and there to organize drawers, closets, and other areas will pay dividends. Those short organizing bursts are most effective if they aren't interrupted or delayed by trips to the store. We also like to save money and use things we already have on hand.

Zip-top plastic bags of various sizes are some of my favorite organizing aids. The snack and sandwich sized ones can store jewelry, cosmetics, office supplies, and just about any small item. They are inexpensive and often need no labels because they're see-through.

Speaking of labels, here is a professional organizer's secret: You really don't need a label maker. Don't get me wrong, label makers are useful, but they require the ongoing expense of the specialized label tape. It also can be time-consuming and tedious to print out labels. Easy alternatives for label material are self-stick mailing labels, adhesive shelf paper cut to label size, or brightly colored duct tape. Armed with a permanent marker and your impromptu label material, you can make a lot of great labels without interrupting your organizing process.

Recycle cardboard boxes for storage containers. Wine boxes, which you can get from your local grocer, are sturdy and typically the same size so they can be stacked easily. The dividers in the box can be removed, or you can use them to store things like large candles or glassware. Shoe boxes make great dresser-drawer dividers for socks or kids clothes.

It's a great idea to be creative and use what you already have around home to store, divide, and conquer when you get these spur-of-the moment organizing bursts. These are just a few ideas. Just keep an eye open for the things that you already have to keep you organized.

Suzette

Ellen
Hankes,
CPO-CD©

Prepare for Santa

I've received a sack full of Christmas lists from children around the world, but Mrs. Claus is concerned the kids will have no room for the new toys. Any ideas to help the kids prepare for Christmas morning?

—Nervous in the North Pole

Don't worry, Santa, I'll help get the word out that parents and kids need to prepare more than just a plate of cookies before you slide down the chimney. I know you're a great delegator and depend on your team of Mrs. Claus and the elves to manage the letters and lists as well as the deliverables and directions. Children and parents can be a part of the team by making sure there will be space for new toys. It's as simple as T-O-Y-S.

- **T is for Take Inventory.** What do the kids want to keep? Are there broken toys you can throw away? Are there some things Mom just can't part with and wants to save as keepsakes?

- **O is for Offer to Others.** Old favorites may find new life with other kids. Make sure the toys and clothing are in good condition before donating to a charity. Rules for donating toys vary, so ask first.

- **Y is for Yesterday.** Kids grow and change. Things they were interested in last year may not be fun anymore. Keepsakes are wonderful, but don't overdo it.

- **S is for Straighten the Space.** An organized play area is more fun for both kids and adults. Is there a way to make more space by moving or repurposing a piece of furniture for storage of toys and games? Labels—either words or pictures—help keep the space neat.

While it may take time and effort, both kids and parents will love the results. There will be more room to enjoy the new things waiting in Santa's sack.

Ellen

Ashley
Kates

Bring on the Bins

My storage area seems to have a lot of miscellaneous items that are just sitting around. It's all stuff I want to keep, but it feels very cluttered and messy. Any ideas on how to manage the mess?

—California Clutter Girl

Storage bins from your local discount store can help you contain the clutter. They come in various sizes and colors to meet your needs. Remember to grab the lid when you purchase your bin, whether you need it or not. If you purchase the same size and type, they will stack nicely in your storage area.

You have all these bins, so now what? Here are some tips to master the art of bin storage:

- Rid your storage area of cardboard boxes. Any items worth keeping can be put in plastic tubs to protect them from dust and water damage.

- Label each bin with a reminder of its contents: pool toys, Christmas lights, kids' clothes.

- Clear bins are a great choice if you would like a visual reminder of what the bin contains. Colored bins might be a better choice if you prefer to have a consistent look to your storage room.

- Slide the bins onto storage racks or shelves. If you don't have shelves, buy stackable bins. Remember, a big bin can get heavy when filled, weighing as much as fifty pounds. It's always a good idea to put the heavy bins on the bottom or have very sturdy shelves.

- Keep the bins you use most often close and accessible. You don't want the bin with the often used sports equipment on the bottom of the stack.

So bring on the bins—and clear the clutter.

Ashley

Cyndy
Salzmann

Frozen Assets

*Before I even get home from work, my family
is texting, "What's for dinner, Mom?" I'm tired,
running a little low on imagination, and need
ideas. What do you suggest?*

—Running on Hungry

I feel your pain! The last thing a girl wants to hear after
a busy day is "What's for dinner?" With just a little
planning, an hour or two, and a small amount of freezer
space, you can answer this question with a smile. Use
these simple recipes to set aside some frozen assets,
and you'll reap the rewards in the busy days to come.

Bonus Burger
This quick and easy recipe from my book *The Occasional
Cook* will yield dinner tonight—and two different meals
to sock away in the freezer. First, prepare a simple
meat mixture:

4 lbs. lean hamburger (or other ground meat)
2 medium onions, chopped
2 tablespoons minced garlic

Brown the meat with the other ingredients. Drain and cool.

Now, here's the fun part. Prepare a family-pleasing "Upside-Down Pizza" for tonight—and stash the other two meals in the freezer.

Upside-Down Pizza

3 to 4 cups meat mixture
2 to 3 cups spaghetti sauce, without meat
2 cups shredded mozzarella cheese
1 can refrigerated crescent rolls
Parmesan cheese, optional

Stir together the meat and the sauce. Spread mixture in a 9x13-inch baking pan. Sprinkle the mozzarella cheese over the meat mixture. Unroll the crescent rolls and lay them over the top. Sprinkle with Parmesan cheese, if desired. Bake at 375° Fahrenheit for 20 to 25 minutes until the sauce is bubbling around the edges and the pastry is golden brown.

While your pizza is baking, use the rest of the meat mixture to whip up these two meals for later.

Sloppy Joes

3 to 4 cups meat mixture
3/4 cup catsup
3 tablespoons mustard
1 tablespoons Worcestershire sauce
2 tablespoons brown sugar
4 to 6 hamburger rolls

1-gallon freezer bags (two)
2-gallon freezer bag (one)

Place all the ingredients, except the rolls, into a 1-gallon freezer bag. Put the rolls in another 1-gallon freezer bag. Place both bags in a 2-gallon freezer bag to make a meal kit. Freeze.

To serve: After thawing, simmer meat mixture 10 minutes. Serve on rolls.

Taco Soup

2 to 3 cups meat mixture
16-oz. can diced tomatoes
16-oz. can diced tomatoes with green chilies
1 package taco seasoning
1 16-oz. can kidney beans (drained and rinsed)
1 16-oz. can corn with liquid
16-oz. can beef broth
1 tablespoon sugar
3 to 4 cups tortilla chips
2 cups cheddar cheese
1-quart freezer bags (one)
1-gallon freezer bags (two)
2-gallon freezer bag (one)

Place all ingredients, except the chips and cheese, in a 1-gallon freezer bag. Place the chips and cheese in separate freezer bags. Place all bags in a 2-gallon freezer bag. Freeze.

To serve: After thawing, simmer soup for 30 minutes. Ladle the soup into bowls and top it with chips and cheese. If desired, serve with sour cream and salsa.

By planning ahead and using your freezer to create frozen assets, you'll have more time to do the things you love.

Cyndy

Diane
Sullivan

Turn Piles into Files

Papers and more papers! The papers are overtaking my home. Is there a way to organize those papers and get them out of my way?

—*Bogg*

Paper management is a source of headaches and stress for many people. Someday we may be a paperless society, but we are a long way from that now. Try creating a file system to corral all those loose papers.

Begin by sorting your papers into piles with like papers together. For example, make a pile of bills, another of reading material, and another of school information. Now make a file folder for each pile, and label it.

Here are some sample general categories to get you started:

- **Bills.** Some people like to divide the month into intervals for bill paying, such as having a file for paying on the fifteenth and another for paying on the thirtieth.

- **To Do.** Include cards and invitations to send, calls to make, and appointments.

- **To File.** This is a holding place for papers that will eventually go to reference or long-term files.

- **To Read.** This is a great place for newsletter or magazine articles.

- **Receipts.** Don't overload this file. Keep only what's needed.

- **Kids' Activities.** In this file, put sports schedules, dance recital information, library hours—you get the idea.

- **Projects.** This file could include information on a home project or a vacation you're planning.

Personally, I include folders such as "To Decide," "Coupons and Gift Cards," "Summer Activities," and "Paid Bills." If you're a detail person, you'll have more folders. If you're a big-picture person, you'll have fewer. Create a file system that you can maintain easily.

Your files may just be the answer for getting you and your paperwork on the same page.

Diane

Sheri
Lukasiewicz

Focus on Finances

We've been married for more than seven years and have just cruised along with neither of us paying much attention to our finances. I know we owe—maybe a lot. How do I start putting things in order?

—Drowning in Denver

You're definitely not alone. One of the things I've learned is that many people are very disorganized when it comes to their finances. In fact, many people have no idea how much debt they have. This type of disorganization is very dangerous to your financial health. It's time to focus and get your financial house in order.

The first thing you need to do is to set up a file for each creditor. Be sure to include past statements, account numbers, interest rates and—most important—balances owed. Be sure to include the following:

- Credit cards
- Car payments
- Home equity loans
- Student loans
- Loans from family members

The next step is to decide on a plan for how you'll pay off your debt. One of the best resources I've found to eliminate debt as soon as possible is what financial guru Dave Ramsey calls a "debt snowball." This plan encourages you to knock out debts from the smallest to the largest. More information as well as many other resources are available on his website at www. daveramsey.com.

The key to keeping your financial house in order is to get organized so you know what you owe—and to whom. In this case, the old saying "Knowledge is power" couldn't ring truer.

Sheri

Donna
Schoeppner

Avoid the Digital Dilemma

I love using all the latest technology, but worry that something might happen to the invaluable memories and records I've saved. Any suggestions?

—Technophile

Because everything stored with the latest technology can be compromised, you can be tech savvy by following a few simple tips:

- If you use digital technology to store photos, video or other keepsakes, be sure to update as technology changes. Otherwise, you'll end up with family memories on a VCR tape, for example, with no way to enjoy it.

- Be sure to back up computer files on a regular basis. A USB flash drive could be used or one of many inexpensive online storage sites. Set a schedule to save as needed, whether it's the first day of each month or each Friday afternoon.

- It's also easy to keep a home inventory with a digital camera. Take several photos in each room. Also take individual photos of more expensive items in case of fire or theft. Keep copies of these photos at a location other than your home or on a photo site.

Keep recording those memories and maintain a backup system to ensure you can continue to enjoy those priceless moments and keep a record of your belongings.

Donna

Traci
Watkins

Shop with a PLAN

I'm the queen of bargain shopping; I never buy anything unless it's on sale. I shop a lot for my family because I'm great at finding a bargain. I don't have a place for everything I buy, so it ends up staying in the bag on the closet floor or the trunk of my car. Do you have suggestions for how to organize new purchases in my home?

—Discount Diva

One in and one out. This means when something comes into the house, something must go out. This will prevent your house from getting stuffed to the seams. If you consistently practice this one shopping guideline, you'll always have a place for something that you want to bring into your home.

As an organizer, when I observe items with price tags and in their original shopping bags, I look a little deeper at household shopping habits. You, too, should explore this if you feel like your life centers around buying things or if others feel that this is the case.

If you agree with any of these following statements, you could be overshopping:

- I feel guilty when I buy something.

- I often hide purchases because I don't want anyone to know I was shopping or because I know I don't need them.

- I spend more than I should.

- I have tried to shop less, but can't seem to stop.

If you are overshopping, it's important to uncover the roots of the issue. Ask yourself why you shop. Is it a quick and easy fix for an emotion you're feeling? Some common feelings that cause overshopping are boredom, anxiety, guilt, shame, stress, and loneliness. You may need professional help from a mental health counselor to uncover the issues.

If this seems like a lot of mumbo-jumbo to you, take another approach. Look at the facts. Do your kids have overflowing closets of clothes that they never wear? Do you have nine scarves of the same color? Write down things that you know you have an over-abundance of in your house, keep the list in your wallet, and resolve not to buy that type of item.

It's also important to determine what makes you want to run to the nearest clearance rack. Do you notice you shop more after watching TV? Record the shows that you enjoy, and fast-forward through commercials so you aren't tempted by the things others want you to purchase. Most importantly, avoid home shopping networks.

Do you get daily deals in emails? They are such good deals, it's hard to say no. Before buying, consider whether you *really* need to buy another discounted item before the offer expires? Also unsubscribe from the catalogs, magazines, websites, or retail newsletters that get you in trouble. Avoid temptations altogether if your wallet is empty or if you noticed that retailers roll a red carpet out for you when you walk in the door.

If you decide to brave the retail jungle, shop with a PLAN.

- **P—Partner**. If you continue to feel like you can't say no to the latest and greatest watch, skirt, gadget, or fabulous pair of wedge-heel strappy sandals, get a shopping buddy. Your shopping partner can keep you on an "affordable" track when you shop together and can hold you accountable when she can't go with you. It's much easier to hear "You really don't need another gold bracelet, do you?" from a trusted friend than from someone that does not have your best interest at heart. Always keep your tags and receipts, and return items that cause you to have "buyer's regret" when you arrive home or when you check in with your shopping partner.

- **L—List.** Make a list before leaving the house, and be sure to have a credible purpose for each item. Don't buy anything that's not on the list.

- **A—Awareness and analysis.** If you find something on the Internet that trips your spending trigger, put it in the Shopping Cart. Wait twenty-four hours and then ask yourself these things: Do I need the item? Where will I put it? Can I afford it? What will happen if I don't buy it? Are there any negative consequences of buying it? Click "Submit Order" only if you can justify the purchase.

- **N—No Credit.** Many people find they spend less when they use only cash for purchases. It's easy to think credit is not really spending your hard-earned money, when in fact you're spending that plus interest.

Finally, spend time thinking about advertising. *Be aware*, because it's *everywhere*. It is hard to dodge a huge and expansive industry specifically created to make us feel inadequate so that we are motivated to go out and purchase items. This is a daily battle for many. Being aware of advertising and its impact on you will make you stronger in the war waged over your wallet.

Traci

Jan
Limpach

Organize Your Christmas Wrapping

During the holiday season, I have this mess of wrapping paper and supplies. I need some help to make my season merry.

—Unwrapped

Along with the hustle and bustle of the holidays, presents are lined up waiting to be wrapped. Whether you use gift bags or wrapping paper, all the embellishments can lead to clutter and mess—tissue paper, gift tags, bows and ribbon, not to mention the always-needed tape, scissors, and pen. Let me offer you some storage ideas for all these supplies.

- Less is more. It's easier to store a smaller quantity of material. That may mean passing up the

90-percent-off, after-Christmas gift wrap sale. You may not even need a scrap of wrapping paper if you rely on gift bags.

- Consider a long, under-the-bed storage bin. This can store long rolls of gift wrap without bending or smashing them.

- Group like items such as ribbons and bows in containers. A pretty basket can hold essentials like scissors, tape, and tags.

- Or use an "over the door" shoe holder with clear pockets that lets you see your supplies. Place tape, ribbons, gift tags, and cards in their own pockets.

- Consider moving your gift wrap station to a less-used space in your home. A card table can easily accommodate supplies and make wrapping easier.

- Set aside a certain time each week to wrap presents. Waiting until Christmas Eve may bring you face-to-face with Santa as he makes his deliveries.

Reduce your holiday wrap clutter and mess—and have a merry one.

Jan

Amy
Tokos

Closet Chic

*Oh my galoshes! My closet is filled to the max.
Every time I open the door, my clothes tumble
out or I have to dig for my shoes. Do you have
any suggestions?*

—Diving Diva

A well-organized closet can be your best fashion accessory. Here are a few of my favorite suggestions to put you on the path to closet chic:

Clothes. One of my favorite tips is to place a Donate basket in the closet. Each morning, when you select an outfit, pull out one you don't wear, and place it in the basket. We all have clothes we plan to wear, but for whatever the reason, they never see the light of day. When your Donate basket is full, promptly give the items to your favorite charity.

Shoes. Next to diamonds, shoes are a girl's best friend. Stay organized by keeping them off the floor on a rack or a shelf. While you might have a couple of pairs of shoes on the floor, try to keep the rest put away. Don't forget, after a successful shoe shopping trip, let go of a pair or two. We organizers refer to this as the "One in, one out" rule.

Accessories. If you have a walk-in closet, it's helpful to keep all your accessories in one area of the closet. This makes it much easier to pull a complete outfit together. If you don't have a walk-in closet, a dresser also works nicely for storing accessories. The key is to keep all the accessories in one place so you don't have to search for that perfect look.

Follow these tips, and you—and your closet—will be très chic.

Amy

Suzette
Gavin

It's Not Your Mom's Cup Hook Anymore

I was at a friend's house the other day, and she was all excited about her new discovery—cup hooks. My mom had cup hooks, but I haven't seen them in years. What's the deal? Is this a new trend?

—Surprised by the Hook

Cup hooks may not be a new trend, but they are a very useful household organizing tool. Mom (and Grandma) knew just how valuable they can be when it comes to using vertical space.

Usually found in the hardware section of your favorite discount or home improvement store, cup hooks are small, metal, C-shaped hooks with a screw attached to one end. They range from a half-inch on up to larger sizes. You may want to buy several sizes because you'll find many uses for them around the house. Just make sure the end of the cup hook that has the threads on it is shorter than the thickness of the wood where you'll install it. Otherwise, when the cup hook is installed, it will poke through the wood. Plan to use wood surfaces to attach the cup hooks for optimum strength.

Here are just a few places where you can use cup hooks to hang many items:

- **Kitchen:** Flat cheese grater, potholders, scissors, measuring spoons, coffee measure, coffee mugs, towels, utensils, pencil on a string

- **Bedroom and bath:** Jewelry, achievement and competition medals and ribbons, hair dryer, belts, scarves, towels, toilet brush

- **Office:** On underside of desk to hide cord clutter, filing cabinet keys

- **Back door and garage:** Keys, tools, reusable shopping bags, extension cord

In fact, anything that has a loop on or hole in it can be hung from a cup hook if it can bear the weight. And don't forget to use cup hooks to hang Christmas stockings.

So, cup hooks aren't a new, exciting trend, but give them a try.

Suzette

Ellen
Hankes,
CPO-CD©

Collector or Hoarder?

My grandma has a lot of stuff that she calls her "collection." Could she be a hoarder?

—Concerned

Hoarding is definitely making news these days and can be a problem for many families. However, there are some important differences between hoarders and collectors.

People with collections enjoy displaying them. Collectors often have one or more areas of their homes where they display their treasured items. Collections are often related by theme or use. For example, a book collection may be displayed on bookshelves, or you may find a seashell collection in a bathroom or bedroom.

Collectors like to show their treasures to friends and relatives, and sometimes the collections even lead to new friendships. People are proud of their carefully assembled collections and are pleased when they acquire another item to add to it. When the size of a collection gets unmanageable, they often trade, sell, or donate duplicates.

Conversely, people who hoard usually have an intense need to acquire items that interest them. And while hoarders may love to add new items, they are extremely averse to getting rid of anything, regardless of its market value. People with these tendencies also feel a lot of embarrassment and may become socially isolated.

An experienced organizer can help a collector like your grandma find new and creative ways to gain control of her treasures. When it comes to hoarding, a specially trained professional organizer, along with mental health counseling, can facilitate long-term change.

Ellen

Ashley
Kates

Perfectly Easy Packing Tips

When I pack my bags for a trip, I have too much of the wrong stuff and forget about the essentials. What's important when I quickly pack my bag?

—Traveling Tess

Whether you're a frequent traveler or someone who takes just a few weekend getaways, it can be tricky to make sure you have everything you need. These tips will help you reach your destination prepared for fun or work:

- Keep your travel bag with all your bathroom necessities packed and ready for a quick get-away. Include toothbrush, toothpaste, travel shampoo/conditioner, body wash, blow dryer, brushes, hair accessories, styling products, medications, and other items you need. With an always-packed-and-ready-to go toiletries kit, you won't forget any basics. Include a small bag for cosmetics so you can select what you need and pack appropriately.

- Just as you have storage compartments in your home, your luggage provides specialized areas for your clothing. To bundle an outfit for packing, fold your shirt, socks (if needed), and underwear into your pants/skirt/shorts. This solution keeps everything grouped together and helps you to locate an outfit with ease. Stack all your grouped-together items, and place them on one side of the suitcase interior, automatically creating a compartment of its own. There's room on the opposite side for your toiletry bag and shoes. Since shoes can be bulky and heavy, try to coordinate clothing so few shoes are needed. Wear the bulkiest pair, like tennis shoes or boots, on the plane.

- Use a tote or something similar for those easy-to-grab items such as boarding passes and snacks. This bag will contain everything you need while you travel, so you don't have to open your suitcase and rummage through everything that is already nicely packed. If you're traveling by air, it's always a good idea to pack an extra outfit in your tote, just in case your luggage is lost.

Enjoy your trip!

Ashley

Cyndy
Salzmann

Memory Keeping

I have five totes of paper and other stuff moldering in my storage room that have special memories attached to them. Any advice on what to keep and what to toss?

—Member Me

This is an excellent question that many struggle to answer. It took a few overflowing totes of my own to come to the conclusion that the real question isn't so much what to keep but what to leave behind. Specifically, what do we want others to remember about us and about our family? What will be our legacy to future generations? I've found that this mindset makes it much easier to muster the courage to toss the dried and dusty corsage from senior prom and to preserve those things that provide an account of the things that really matter.

Here are some ideas to get you thinking beyond photo albums:

- If you like to scrapbook, I encourage you not to stop with cute photos and kitschy souvenirs. Take time to record the feelings, blessings, and lessons connected to these events.

- Consider sharing a well-loved book with future generations. Take the time to jot a note on one of the inside pages about why this particular book is important to you. My son tells me one of the best gifts he received is the Bible I passed along to him, marked up with the lessons God taught me during eight years of Bible study.

- Certain objects can convey a powerful meaning when the story is shared. Attach a written account and photo to the back of a special piece of art that explains why it's special.

- If you like to write, exploit that passion. Keep a journal of your thoughts. Or write letters to family members that include more than the current weather conditions and family ailments. And for those who count faith in God as an important part of life, don't forget to record your testimony to pass on to those you love.

Don't be afraid to keep items that show your warts. Otherwise, you might as well leave behind a Barbie doll—perfect, but also cold, plastic, and lifeless. Instead, give future generations a peek into the heart of a real person—who occasionally has a bad hair day.

Cyndy

Diane Sullivan

Is It a Basket or a Table?

My apartment is so small. Do you have ideas on how to stretch my budget and get more storage?

—Cramped

You can get more storage and save some money by having dual-functioning items. Here are a few ideas:

- A wicker basket with a lid can serve both as an end table and as storage for extra blankets.

- Many ottomans come with built-in storage.

- A coffee table with drawers can help conceal the items in the living area.

- Consider a platform bed with drawers.

- A dining-room buffet could become a home office credenza.

- Use a pretty tablecloth to conceal large totes with lids.

- Make a charging station by punching holes in the back of a small drawer unit that can be put on a shelf. The charger goes in drawer with the cord coming out the back.

- Tote bags can be mini-storage units. For example, keep your volunteer information in a tote bag. You can stow the bag under the desk until you need it for a meeting.

When purchasing a new piece of furniture, challenge yourself to identify pieces that are functional and have storage potential. You will save both space and money.

Diane

Sheri
Lukasiewicz

Peace-of-Mind File

My husband is very busy with work, so I handle all the family finances. What if something happens to me? I don't want leave him clueless.

—Planning Ahead

Your situation is not uncommon, and you're wise to think ahead. Generally one person in a household is in charge of financial matters and bill paying. If that person is suddenly unable to perform those tasks, someone else has to step in. Knowing that financial information is readily available lends a degree of peace and confidence to an otherwise stressful time.

Every family needs a place to store important financial information. This can be a box, pocket portfolio, or expanding file. Here are some items to include:

- A list of financial websites with login information including usernames, passwords, and answers to security questions.

- Bank names and corresponding account numbers for checking and savings

- Information on investment accounts, including 401K, pension, mutual funds, etc.

- Account numbers and payment information for loans (mortgage, auto, credit cards, etc.)

- List of insurance policies with contact information

- Copy of your will

Store this information in a safe place, and make sure you let a trusted family member or friend know where you keep it.

This is a project you can do with little or no cost other than an investment of time. And what better gift could you give to a loved one?

Sheri

Donna
Schoeppner

Turn the Car Around

I'm constantly on the go. Between me and my kids, the car is always a mess. Any ideas for me and my constant companion, the car?

—Not Speeding

There are numerous car organizers available to help keep your car in shipshape condition.

One of my favorites is the over-the-seat organizer for kids, which hangs on the front seat and faces the back seat. These keep their favorite traveling items and toys in place and off the floor. Here are a few more:

- Organizers that slip onto a visor can hold CDs or your registration and insurance information.
- Car trash bins can contain all those snack wrappers and empty drink bottles.

- Trunk organizers can hold emergency items like jumper cables, a first-aid kit, a blanket and a small tool kit.

When I bought my first car, my dad created a tool kit for me. I still have that same one today and use it periodically. This kit includes basic tools, but also many other useful items that I might need a pinch:

- Bungee cord
- String
- Wire coat hanger
- Small
- Ice scraper
- Bottle opener
- Flashlight
- Plastic bag

Believe it or not, I used that coat hanger and flashlight one evening when I dropped my keys down a street grate. It was both heartening and amusing to see the number of people who gathered to help fish them out.

Whether you spend minutes or hours in your car each day, a few of these organizing products will help create a mess-free vehicle.

Donna

Traci
Watkins

Your Garage—Reclaim the Space

My garage makes me want to jump in my car and take off as fast as I can. It's a disaster, so I'm looking for some organizing ideas. Can you help?

—Garage Girl

Yes, I can help. A garage can be a great extended living space, storage space, and activity area. Given all these uses, it's almost like the inside of a house, but it doesn't have the walls that separate it into rooms. A quick way to get the most use out of your garage is to set it up in "zones."

Here are some zone examples:

- **Gardening/yard equipment.** Place this zone near an outside door. This creates easy access for use and facilitates returning of items.

- **Sports equipment and outside toys.** This is another zone that can be near the outside door. Consider hanging or shelving the equipment at a family-friendly height.

- **Tools and project supplies.** Whether it's woodworking or car repair, hobbies come with a lot of tools and supplies. Having everything together in a zone makes it easy to find and put away the needed items. This means less time searching and more time enjoying your hobby.

- **Chemicals.** Keep these in a secure cabinet. Paints, gardening chemicals, and pesticides need to be keep away from children and pets.

- **Recycling and trash.** Place containers for these items where they are most convenient. Having bins just a few steps from the kitchen makes throwing things out easier. And try not to let recyclables and trash pile up.

Setting up zones can make your garage more functional as well as more fun. You may even end up with a new parking space for a car.

Traci

Jan
Limpach

Tackle Procrastination

I keep putting things off. I know I'm procrastinating, but I can't get motivated to tackle my to-do list. I need help...tomorrow.

—*Couch Potato*

Procrastination is a big deal to many of us. We aren't motivated or interested enough to address things we know we should do. It's like we tell ourselves, "You can't make me do that." The fact is that every fifth person identifies herself as a chronic procrastinator. That means you're not alone. Many people are missing out on life because of procrastination.

If a task seems overwhelming, identify small steps to get it started. Work through these small steps in short increments of time. For example, work at cleaning out the basement in small chunks rather than devoting an entire weekend to the task. Before you know it, the big job will be completed. Some people compare this to eating an elephant. How do you eat an elephant? One bite at a time.

Another approach is to include a friend while you work on a project. A person who is frank and supportive is good in this role. If you schedule your helper to come over while you clean out your closet or garage, she can hold you accountable and keep you moving. This makes it easier to stay focused, and you have someone to celebrate with afterward.

Procrastination is a complex subject that you might want to read more about. Sound habits like the two ideas above can help you get motivated and on your way.

Jan

Amy
Tokos

Are You Up for a Camping Trip?

My friend is trying to convince me to take a family camping trip. Planning for a weekend in the woods is overwhelming. Help.

—Anxious Anna

Campers love to tell you how much fun it is to go camping. As a mother of four, it took me many years—ten years to be exact—to overcome the daunting task of planning a family camping trip. The secret is definitely in the planning.

Here are four ever-so-easy tips for planning a successful camping trip:

1. Write down your meal plan for the weekend. Keep the menu choices simple with few ingredients that will travel well. Our family favorite is Walking Tacos, which use all the familiar taco ingredients except for the tortilla or shell, which is replaced by small bags of nacho chips. Few ingredients are needed, and we save on dishes by serving Walking Tacos in the chip bags.

2. Make two lists—one for shopping and one for packing. Go through your menu and include the ingredients on your shopping list and the equipment—like pots, pans, spatula, and cooking spray. Do this for each meal, and you'll be sure to have marshmallows for your s'mores.

3. Now add the camping essentials to the packing list. Write down everything you think of, including the obvious, like the tent. When you complete your packing list, put it on the computer. This will be helpful for your next camping trip (if there is one).

4. Allow time to do cooking and prep work at home. Plastic bags are great for anything you can slice and dice. I make the meat for the Walking Tacos ahead of time and freeze it. The frozen meat packages helps keep the cooler cold.

If you're stumped in your planning, search the Internet for camping lists, meal ideas, and simple recipes.

With the planning and packing done, all that's left is enjoying the outdoors. Have fun camping!

Amy

Ellen
Hankes,
CPO-CD©

Organize Like the Moss Rose

When I wake up each morning, I already feel like I'm behind. Any advice to help me avoid the inevitable morning mania?

—Dreading the Dawn

Would you believe I learned a powerful lesson about organizing from the tiny moss rose in my garden? Here's what the moss rose understands that we often fail to remember: Fold it up at night. Some moss rose varieties close in the evening and reopen when the conditions are right the following day.

What do we need to do to fold things up at night? Of course, you'll have your own list, but here are some examples:

- Put unfinished paperwork in a folder.
- Gather the toys.
- Clear the counter top so it's ready for the morning rush.
- Start the dishwasher.
- Lay out clothes for the following day.
- Plan the next day's meals.
- Call/text/email someone you care about.
- Count your blessings.

Preparing for the following day pays big dividends. The result will be a smaller step, a joy shared, and a more organized day to follow. Your day will be filled with all sorts of good, simple things—just like the moss rose.

Ellen

Ashley
Kates

Smooth Your Move

My move is looming and I know I'm going to be living out of boxes until I get settled. I'm totally stressed thinking about how I'm going to find my stuff when I need it.

—Miserable Mover

Anyone who has moved knows the stress of rushing to pack followed by the drawn-out process of unpacking at the new location. Here are three powerful tips to help make this not-so-fun task a little easier:

- **Like with like.** Pack similar items in each room together. Organizers call this placing like items with like. Leave the boxes that correspond with that room in that space.

- **Home sweet *new* home.** When packing to move, make sure all items for one room are in the boxes they need to be in at the new location. For example, place all your bathroom items together in a box or two.

- **Pare down.** Set aside the things you want to donate or throw away. If you do this before you move, it will make the transition into the new space go more smoothly.

- **Log logic.** After packing the contents of each room, create a log. Label the boxes with the name of the room and a consecutive number. For example: Kitchen 1-10, Bathroom 11-13, etc. In the log, write a brief note about what is in each box. The log entry for box Kitchen 1 might say "towels and placemats." This creates an easy-to-find list for the "I need this now!" moment, so you won't have to open fifty boxes to search for it. Once you get to the new location, you can go back through your log and be sure the boxes go in the correct rooms.

When you pack in this way, if you're delayed in unpacking, you can identify which box has your favorite bubble bath or favorite pair of shoes without going through them all.

Moving is not much fun, but you can make it manageable with these simple tips.

Ashley

Cyndy
Salzmann

Back-to-School Checklist

Don't tell my kids but I'm already thinking about the first day of school and all I need to do this summer to be ready for fall. How can I avoid the last-minute rush?

—School Mom

My dear, you're an organizer's dream! It's great that you're inspired to get a head start on back-to-school chores. Here's a checklist to send you to the head of the class:

- Make necessary doctor and dentist appointments.

- Clean out the kids' closets and make a list of what they'll need for next year.

- Watch for clothing sales and tax-free holidays.

- Set up carpooling and any needed after-school care.

- Schedule back-to-school haircuts.

And a couple of weeks before school starts, do this:

- Check the school website for forms to fill out and school supply lists.

- Purchase school supplies.

- Ease the kids into their school-night bedtime routine.

- Stock up on school lunch supplies and after-school snacks.

Once again, my dear, you get an "A for effort" from this organizer.

Cyndy

Diane
Sullivan

File It or Not

I'm paralyzed when I try to decide whether to keep or toss the papers that come into my home. How do I know what to keep and what to toss?

—*Paper Princess*

I agree. Deciding which papers to keep and toss can sometimes be overwhelming. Here is a simple "FILE IT" test that will help you make decisions. Apply the test to each piece of paper.

F—Will you need this paper in the **future**?

I—Is this **item** a one and only?

L—Are there negative consequences if you **lose** this document?

E—Is this paperwork **essential**?

I—Does your **intuition** tell you to keep it?

T—Did you say no to every question? If so, then you can **toss** the piece of paper.

If you said yes to even one of the questions, the paper is worth keeping and placing in a file. Once you get going with the "FILE IT" test, you may find that it helps you make decisions.

Diane

Sheri
Lukasiewicz

Bidding a Collection Good-Bye

I have a huge collection of angel figurines that were given to me when I was a kid. The collection once meant a lot to me, but I've grown up and now I don't know what to do with all these figurines. Can you give me some advice?

—Heaven's Child

Let me share my personal collection story. Years ago, I collected Coca-Cola memorabilia. The collection started with the oh-so-adorable polar bear, and it morphed into all things Coke: decorative tins, ornaments, playing cards, signs, and even Coke bottles from Mexico. You get the picture.

Back then, I had space to proudly display my collection. Seventeen years and several moves later, my home no longer had the space. Therefore the memorabilia was all stored in boxes, and I had no desire to display it.

That all recently changed. My dad, whom I call Pop, underwent months of hospitalization, leaving him with mountainous bills. A fundraising benefit to help pay his bills included an auction with many donated items—including my Coke collection.

I have immeasurable satisfaction knowing that I helped Pop, whom I cherish so much more than those objects. I have had no remorse whatsoever about the loss of my collection.

Think about the options for your collection. Perhaps you know someone who would delight in it as you once did. Maybe there is a cause or charity that could benefit from it. Would selling the items be a blessing to your family?

You have a choice to make. Give yourself permission to edit the collection from your life.

Sheri

Donna
Schoeppner

Controlling Closet Chaos

I really dislike even stepping foot in my closet.
I can never seem to find what I'm looking for.
Any ideas on how to organize my wardrobe?

—Hanging Around

Your closet can become a welcoming space with two simple steps.

1. **Item.** First, separate by item. Hang all like items together: pants in one section; skirts, shirts and dresses each in their own designated space.

2. **Color.** Second, within each group of items, sort by color from light to dark. It's much easier to look through one color than it is to search the entire closet for a particular item.

While it does take a few extra seconds longer to put away clothes, the rewards make it worthwhile. Also, this is a great way to see what you may be lacking in your wardrobe and what you might want to skip on your next shopping trip. By using these suggestions, you'll save time, space and maybe even a little money.

Donna

Traci
Watkins

Planning for Pets

My pets are like members of the family. And, like kids, they have accumulated lots of stuff. Any ideas for keeping this stuff under control?

—*Pet Lover*

Indeed, pets are part of many households. Whether you have a dog, a cat, a fish, or even a gecko, these little critters will claim their own space in your home. With a little planning and organization, your pet will have everything it needs to be happy.

Think about your pet's daily needs and store those things at their point of use.

- Pet food can be stored close to where the animals are fed. Plastic or metal storage containers keep the animals from snacking between meals. If your pet needs daily medication, keep it in a safe area where you'll remember to use it.

- Keep a basket in the areas where toys tend to collect. This makes a nightly toy pickup quick and easy.

- Keep everything you need for walking your dog near the door. This includes leashes, potty bags, treats, and a towel for rainy days. If you groom your dog outside, you may also want to keep a brush by the door. Store a lint roller near the front door if pet hair on your clothing is an issue.

Other things are needed for pets on a less frequent basis and can be stored in appropriate areas.

- Keep a file folder just for your pet. You will always know where to find information on training, boarding, vaccination, and veterinary visits.

- Pets like to go on outings and trips just like their owners. Keep leashes, carriers, and traveling supplies together in a storage area.

- Keep the bathing supplies near where you wash the pet. This includes pet shampoo and towels.

When you consider the point of use for your pet supplies and equipment, it's easier to make space for your pet in the home. Hey, maybe you can even train your pet to pick up after itself.

Traci

Jan
Limpach

Never-Ending Laundry

Laundry at my house seems to be a never-ending process. I need ideas on making this task a little less painful.

—Sophie Suds

Laundry is a fact of life. Sometimes it's helpful to be thankful for the people in your life who create all that laundry. But whether you have four loads a week or forty, it's sometimes a dreaded chore. My family has three to four loads of laundry a day.

To get the clothes from dirty to done, there are several steps: collect, sort, wash, dry, fold, and put away. To make it easy to collect dirty clothes, have a clothes basket or hamper readily available.

Sort items into whites, colors, jeans, towels, and bedding. This reduces the wear and tear on the fabrics and helps the process move along. You may find a laundry sorter helpful. When a section of the laundry sorter is full, it's time to put that load in the washer.

The quicker you get the items out of the dryer, the better the clothes will look. Hang and fold the clothes as soon as possible. Each family member can take his or her folded and hanging clothes and put them away.

Sometimes this process seems to take a lot of time, but I want to challenge that thought. Start a timer next time you fold a load of clothes to find out how long it really takes. The last time I timed myself, it took less than five minutes, which was only a commercial break during my favorite TV show.

Some people choose to do laundry every day, while others find it more helpful to wash once a week. Do what works best for your schedule. If you do your laundry more often, you may find that you need fewer clothing items and linens.

Post a sheet of laundry directions near the washer so each person in the house can find that information when doing laundry. This encourages independence in your household and hopefully prevents pink underwear.

Jan

Amy
Tokos

Kids Love Their Stuff

My preschooler's room is always a cluttered mess. How can I keep my messy toddlers from becoming messy teenagers?

—Mom of Toddlers in Training

We all know kids love their stuff. And at two feet tall, they think the floor is the best place to keep it. Here are some tips to keep kid spaces from taking over the house:

- **Set up zones** in the room for different activities such as sleeping, dressing, playing, and reading. A reading zone might have a bookshelf and child-sized chair.

- **Group like items together**. A play area could have a bin for blocks and a bin for toy cars. In the dressing area, place a mirror with a basket next to it that holds a brush and hair accessories.

- **Get everything off the floor.** The floor should not be a permanent home for anything. It's especially important in a kid's room that *everything* has a place.

- **For children under three**, I recommend cleaning out most of the room by yourself and then bringing him or her in to help. This gets the toddler involved but makes the project less overwhelming. To minimize temper tantrums, remove items in advance that you plan to donate or trash.

- **Children over the age of three** need to work *with you* to organize their rooms. I always recommend that you ask the questions and let your child make the decisions. For example, after you've gathered all their books, you might say, "I like to keep my books close to my bed where I read. Where would you like to set up yours?" It's important to honor their preferences.

Letting kids manage their own space helps teach valuable life lessons—and their future college roommate will be extremely grateful.

Amy

Suzette
Gavin

Hang It Up

I look at those pictures of beautiful closets with fancy hangers. What kind of hangers do you recommend?

Hooked

Those showcase closets are beautiful. I know what you mean about the uniform hangers. Many featured closets have only wood hangers. Some of my organizing colleagues have a preference for the anti-slip velvet hangers. I personally advise fitting the type of hanger to the specific clothing article. Here's how I use various types of hangers:

- **Molded wooden hangers.** Use these for blazers and tailored jackets when it's important to keep the shape of the collar and shoulders.

- **Pant hangers with wide clamps.** Sometimes referred to as trouser hangers, these are wooden clamps about eleven inches long. The cuff portion of the pants is clamped and the pants hang from there. No creases! Hang skirts by the waistband with these hangers. Make sure you have a long enough area so pants or long skirts can hang their full length if you use this system. A variation is the pant hanger with two clips.

- **Suit hangers.** Any outfit with a coordinating top and bottom can be hung on a suit hanger. This combination hanger has space for hanging a jacket or top as well as a skirt or pants. This is especially helpful to conserve closet space.

- **Anti-slip hangers.** These velvety hangers are great for garments with straps, tank tops, and lingerie. Slippery, sheer apparel stays on these hangers, which hold in the gentlest way. You may want to apply non-slip strips to your favorite hangers to get a similar effect.

- **Plastic tube hangers.** Use half-inch diameter molded hangers for sweat pants or turtlenecks. I prefer these molded hangers over wire hangers because they don't leave shoulder bumps or dents in the fabric.

- **Wire hangers.** While you may not find wire hangers in picture-perfect closets in magazines, they are cheap and readily available. If you use a laundry service, remember that they will take them back for reuse.

- **Multiplier hangers.** Think one space with multiple items hanging from that hook. There are skirt hangers and pant hangers that accommodate a half dozen garments in one space. While these may be space-efficient, they can be hard to maintain.

- **Accessory hangers.** You can find specialty hangers for scarves, belts, purses, and just about anything that goes in your closet.

My recommendation is to use a variety of hangers. The size of your closet, the quantity and type of your clothes, and your budget will determine what kinds of hangers are best for you.

Suzette

Ellen
Hankes,
CPO-CD©

Hold the Reindeer! We're Not Ready for the Holidays

During the holiday season my to-do list is as long as Santa's gift list. With so many things to do, I have no time for myself. Help!

—*Going Going Gone*

It's really difficult to keep up with the whirl of holiday activities and still have time to enjoy the magic. Don't let the reindeer start before you're ready! Allot time to maintain your priorities during the holiday season. Here are some ways to maximize the final hours before the holiday celebrations:

- Take a deep breath.
- Call, email, or text an old friend.
- Listen to your favorite Christmas music.
- Thank all store personnel that you encounter.
- Make room for another around the dinner table.
- Share with others who need warmth, food, clothing, or shelter.
- Read the verses and notes on the Christmas cards you receive.
- Call your neighbors and tell them how much you enjoy their holiday lights.
- Buy premade cookie dough, and let the family make their favorite cookie shapes.

With a little modification, these mini-celebrations can be done all year long. These efforts can take little time and yet pay big heartfelt rewards.

Ellen

Ashley
Kates

Climbing the Walls

I've run out of room to store my stuff. Do you have any creative ideas for small spaces?

—Squeezed in St. Louis

When you've run out of space, it's time to climb the walls. Go vertical!

No matter the room or the size, adding shelving will optimize your space. And shelving doesn't have to be boring or detract from your décor. Whether it's an office, laundry room, or living room, you can design the space as simply or as elegantly as you like by adding decorative baskets, storage bins, or other accessories.

Instead of a short shelf unit, use a tall one. You will double the storage without using an inch more floor space. Tuck a cute set of hooks or a hanging shoe rack behind a door to take advantage of even more vertical space.

By climbing the walls, you'll open up the floor and keep your things from getting lost in the clutter.

Ashley

Cyndy
Salzmann

Spring Cleaning Simplified

After a long winter, I feel like my house needs a breath of fresh air. My grandma called it spring cleaning, but I don't have a clue how to do it.

—Warm Weather Wanda

I agree! There's just something about spring that brings out my inner neatnik and makes me want to throw open the windows and knock down some cobwebs. Here are some of my favorite spring cleaning tips for both those who know their way around the cleaning aisle and those who might be a bit "domestically challenged":

1. Clear away the clutter. Make a sweep around the room with a laundry basket; put all the things

that don't belong in the room into the basket. Put away the contents when you're finished with the room. Or better yet, ask your family to put their own stuff away.

2. Once you've cleared the clutter, you're ready to clean. The most important thing to remember is to work from the top down and from inside to outside. This way, you won't get what you just cleaned dirty again. Use a duster with an extendable handle for reaching above window and door frames and into corners. This also works well for dusting books and ceiling fans.

3. Move on to surfaces such as furniture and countertops. Use an all-purpose cleaner to remove dirt and grime. Protect furniture and other wood surfaces with a coat of lemon oil.

4. Finish the room by vacuuming the carpet or mopping the floor.

Now here's the most important part of successful spring cleaning: Reward your hard work with a relaxing lunch or a long soak in a fragrant bath. After all, a girl's gotta have fun!

Cyndy

Diane
Sullivan

Teeny Tiny Closet Tip

I love everything in my closet. My closet is also overloaded, overcrowded, and overstuffed. What is the best way to decide what clothes I want to live with and what clothes I can live without?

—Fashionista

Here is the best tip that I have found to help keep a closet functioning in the most efficient manner: hang all your hangers backward. What I mean by this is to have the tips of the hanger tips facing you instead of the closet wall.

After you wear and launder an item, hang it back in the closet with the hanger facing the usual way with the hanger tip facing the closet wall. At the end of the season, the clothes hanging backward will be the ones you didn't wear all season.

Donate the clothes you don't wear to your favorite charity, and you'll have a closet full of clothes you love and use.

Diane

Sheri
Lukasiewicz

Failure to Launch

I have a few projects that need to get done, but day after day I find excuses not to even start. What should I do?

—Unmotivated

What you have is a failure to launch. You make a plan on how and when you're going to do it, but you can't seem to bring your plan to fruition. You keep shelving the project for some unexplained reason. Do you find yourself just orbiting around it? Going around in circles rather than taking off and getting it done?

So, how do you get off the launch pad? Try one of these motivational techniques to see if it will propel you to success.

- Find the reason for the project, and buy into it. Ask yourself if the project is worthy of your valuable time. If it's less important than the time and effort it will take, it will continually sink to the bottom of your priority list.

- Break down a big project into smaller attainable tasks. For example, painting a room involves selecting a color, buying the paint, assembling materials, prepping the room, painting, and admiring your finished work.

- Estimate the time a project will take. It may not require as much time as you thought. Don't set aside a whole day to work at clearing out your kitchen cabinets. Allot a half-hour to do one section a day.

- Create or capitalize on urgency. Weekend company or having the bunko group over on Thursday evenings may spur you into action.

- Find a buddy. Do you have someone who can help you get the job done? Perhaps a daughter or friend? The buddy system can work wonders for keeping you focused and accountable for the scheduled task.

Find the motivation that makes you tick, and you'll soon rocket to the Land of Accomplishment. It's a grand place, and there's room for you there.

Sheri

Donna
Schoeppner

Check Your Shoes at the Door

We're always late for everything because the whole family searches everywhere for their shoes. Any ideas to get us out the door faster?

—Scrambling to Find a Mate

Shoes tend to end up in every room of the house. Get organized *and* keep your house cleaner by creating a shoe zone near the door you use most often. A shoe organizer with slots for each family member is an easy solution. Keep the shoes you all wear most often in this area, and swap out shoes as the seasons change.

It's more likely the footwear will find its home when stored where you use it. Plus, it's less work, because shoes don't need to be toted to bedroom closets. You also won't track in who-knows-what on the bottom of your shoes.

When you keep shoes organized by the door, your family will no longer scramble for them when they leave the house. And the bonus: you'll spend less time cleaning your floors.

Donna

Traci
Watkins

Conquering Cupboard Mayhem

I love to cook, but chaos has replaced creativity in my kitchen. Even making a batch of cookies turns into a game of Where's Waldo?

—*Rachel Wreck*

Relax! There are some things you can do that will make a big difference in your kitchen. Here are a few ideas for taming the chaos:

- **Organize your kitchen by activity**. This will cut down on steps and make things easy to find. For example, put coffee, filters, and mugs in the cabinet above your coffeemaker.

- **Take advantage of unused space**. You only have so many shelves and cabinets in a kitchen. By placing wire shelves in them, you double the storage area. In deep corner cabinets, use turntables to see and reach items easily. Turntables are also great in regular-depth cabinets for storing canned food and spices. Some people prefer stair-step cabinet inserts for these items. Plastic containers are also helpful to corral small things such as cookie cutters, sauce packets, and pot lids.

- **Repackage dry goods.** Containers help make the most of your available space and also help to keep your dry goods fresh and free of pests. I recommend containers that are clear, airtight, stackable, and square or rectangular. Be sure to label the containers and include cooking instructions, as needed.

- **Speaking of labels...** Labeling in the kitchen can be very helpful. If it's hard to find things in your fridge or cupboards, consider putting labels on the shelves. This will also make it easier for others to return things to their proper places

An easy way to accomplish this is to organize one cabinet at a time. By the time you're through, your kitchen will be the creative space you desire.

Traci

Jan
Limpach

Savvy Solutions for School Supplies

I like to stock up on extra school supplies when they are on sale but often forget where I've stashed them when my kids need something— and end up buying duplicates. And don't even get me started on the backpacks littering the floor.

—Buried in No. 2 Pencils

First, congratulations for thinking ahead. Buying a few extra supplies often saves time and money. The problem, as you've found, is keeping track of your "inventory" so it doesn't get out of control. Here are a couple of ideas that will send you and your child to the head of the class:

Limited storage space. Try using an over-the-door shoe organizer with clear, plastic pockets. These handy organizers can hold all sorts of things: tape, glue sticks, notepads, staples, pens, and pencils. Since you can see what you have at a glance, you'll be less likely to buy duplicates and you'll save yourself a last-minute run to the store.

Backpacks. To keep your kids' backpacks from littering the house, they need a home. You might install hooks on the back of the door or create a cubby for each child similar to the one they use at school. Or try one of my favorites— a product called the Over-the-Door Back Pack Rack by Jokari, which can accommodate up to three fully loaded backpacks. Now, if you want to get really organized, put together backpacks for different activities such as music, sports, or special interests.

With these systems, kids can count on having what they need for school when they need it. This adds up to less stress for the whole family. Helping your children learn to be organized empowers them to have more productive days and form more productive lives.

Jan

Amy
Tokos

It's the Simple Things

My husband plans our family vacation
more like the Amazing Race than a time to
reconnect and relax. How do I get him to slow
down so I don't feel like I need a vacation
when we get home?

—Teary Traveler

Sometimes when we're planning vacations, we get caught up in doing big-ticket things like amusement parks. But the simple things can be just as much fun— and more relaxing.

Recently, while we were planning a family vacation to the Grand Canyon, I had a light-bulb moment. We had a long itinerary of things we wanted to see and do along the way. Unfortunately, that also had my dear hubby seeing a lot of dollar signs. So we decided to save money on our nightly accommodations.

Camping in tents was mentioned, but it seemed like way too much work to pitch a tent every night. In other words, I screamed, "No way!"

In the end, we reached a compromise. We decided to stay at KOA Kampgrounds in their Kamping Kabins and chose a small log cabin with two rooms. One area had two sets of bunk beds for our four kids and the second room had a double bed for us. The cabin had electricity and heat, but no running water. We had to walk to the community bathrooms and showers. I would characterize the cabin accommodation as a small step up from tent camping.

Now for my light-bulb moment. Our first night in the cabin, we cooked dinner on the fire, roasted marshmallows, and took a walk. One of my kids said, "Mom, I love this place. It's better than that hotel with the water park." This made me realize that while our weekends at the water park were exciting, my family thinks the simple things are a lot of fun too. It's really all about being together. And that "Kamping" trip is still one of our family's favorite memories.

So my best advice is, take a look at your itinerary and see where you can simplify. You'll come back more relaxed, refreshed—and reconnected.

Amy

Diane
Sullivan

Organize Your Health Records

*My file cabinets are bulging with medical
records. What papers do I really need to keep?*

—Fairly Healthy

It's hard to know which medical records to keep and
how long to retain them. Everything looks so official.

Let's take a look at what information you may have
in your files. Some of this information may be kept in
electronic format and some as paper copies. You can
find several different types of forms and lists on the
Internet that can help you record your medical history, or you can use your own notes. Make a list of the
following:

- **Medications and supplements.** Include the name, dosage, and how much per day and for how long. Also include all supplements and over-the-counter drugs you're taking. If you keep a list on the computer, you can easily update it as needed and print a current one when you visit the doctor.

- **Pharmacies.** Write down the names, addresses, and telephone number of any pharmacies you use. This is helpful when a prescription needs to be called in by your medical provider.

- **Medical history.** Include a short medical history, including past surgeries or major problems, doctors' names and telephone numbers, immunizations, allergies, and insurance information. Don't forget each member of the family. Keep these records forever.

- **Medical power of attorney.** This ensures your wishes are enforced if you're unable to make those decisions. This is a legal document and should be available for as long as it is in effect.

- **Medical family tree.** This should include any family medical history and genetic predispositions to certain diseases. Keep these records forever.

- **Doctors and medical professionals**. Keep a list of those you see, including their names, addresses, and telephone numbers. While these may change from time to time, it will be a helpful resource later if you need to get medical records from a previous health care provider.

- **Insurance.** You receive Explanation of Benefits (EOB) forms from your insurance company if you have medical expenses that are submitted to insurance. Check with your insurance company to see if your records are available online; if so, you may not have to keep paper copies. I suggest that you keep paper EOBs for one calendar year until you file your taxes for that year, in case you become eligible for a tax deduction.

- **Proof of paid bills.** In case of a payment dispute, it is helpful to retain proof of payment such as a check or credit card statement.

Here's wishing you good health and an organized health record.

Diane

Suzette
Gavin

Keep the Memories and Store the Holiday Décor

I love the holidays! The more decorations the merrier...until I try to put them away. What do you suggest?

—In the Spirit

It definitely is more fun to get out the holiday decorations than to put them away. Make it easy to stow the festive things, and that part can be more fun. Here are a few hints to make putting away the holiday decorations a bit easier:

- When storing holiday decorations, remember you'll get these items out only once a year. Store them in an out-of-the-way place like under the basement stairs or high on a shelf in the basement or garage. If you have an attic that has a storage area, this is also an option. Candles may melt in a hot attic, so store them somewhere else.

- Create a zone for each holiday. It may be as simple as a box of Halloween decorations or an entire closet dedicated to storing décor for a specific holiday.

- Label your holiday decorations with the years that you use them. If the sweet Valentine decorations haven't been used for a few years, it may be time to move them on to someone who can use them. When you set up your decorations, donate the ones that you don't use anymore. You will have more room for storing the decorations you do use.

Celebrate the holidays. Give your decorations a home that they can return to year after year.

Suzette

Ellen
Hankes,
CPO-CD©

Is It a Collection or Just Clutter?

My son is livid with me because I threw away some of his rock collection. I thought it was just clutter, but obviously I was wrong. What's the difference between clutter and a collection?

—Hit Rock Bottom

People of all ages struggle with collections that become clutter. As your son builds his collection, he is expressing his interests at this stage of his life. He will collect rocks for reasons that are important to him. Each rock may come from a special place or be a unique color.

As with anyone who is building a collection, it's important to have a special place designated to contain or display it. It may start in a shoe box and eventually grow to fill a display case.

New interests may dictate how the collection grows or gets left behind in pursuit of other interests. Our organizing clients often show us collections that are frozen in time. Your son's rock collection may eventually lose its novelty for him, and that's when it would become clutter.

Consider putting the collection in storage as new interests compete for precious space. Or have your son place his rocks in a garden. An adult may want to give a special collection to someone who wants it, donate it to charity, or sell it on eBay.

Once your son's rock collection is contained, it will be there to share with family and friends as a collection, not clutter.

Ellen

Ashley
Kates

Purge and Donate

I have a lot of things to donate—suits, books, glasses. Any suggestions?

—Urge to Purge

As matter of fact, yes! We organizers refer to going through things as "purging." Purging is only half the battle. Trying to find a good home for the things we no longer can use is the second half. Even too-small shoes and dreamy travel guides are useful to someone else, and it may be easy to decide to sell, donate, or trash them. But where does a girl go with business clothing, books, and eyeglasses?

- **Business clothing.** Women's shelters and groups such as Dress for Success (www.dressforsuccess. org) accept clothing such as business suits, dress shoes, and accessories that women in transition can use to make a good impression in job interviews. Check with local groups to learn what they will accept. Gently used items of clothing, bags, jewelry, or shoes are popular needs. You will help tomorrow's businesswomen in need of the professional look at less than executive prices.

- **Books**. Like many people, I saved most of my books pertaining to my college major in hopes they would be of some use in the future. The reality: I've never opened those textbooks. So pick a few favorites if you *must* keep some. Donate or sell the rest to a local library, school, or college, or through an online used bookstore. This works with all books. Don't overlook novels, children's books, and even magazines.

- **Eyeglasses**. When your prescription changes, you have an extra pair of glasses. Trends change, and so do our tastes in eyewear styles. When you want to get rid of old glasses, check with your vision center. They often donate eyewear directly to local service clubs for needy seniors and others. Don't forget to toss in your old reading glasses and sunglasses. Make sure that your backup pair of glasses doesn't accidentally end up in the donation box.

With a little creativity and a quick Internet search, you can find good homes for just about anything.

Ashley

Cyndy
Salzmann

Purge Your Piles

Every flat surface in my home has a pile...or two... or twenty. I even have grocery sacks filled with paper in my closet. Can you help me get a grip on all this paper?

—Polly Doesn't Want More Paper

The most common question I'm asked as a professional organizer is how to manage all the paper that comes into homes and offices. My advice is almost always the same: Make it easy to deal with paper as soon as it arrives. Don't let papers pile up.

Here are my favorite tips:

- **Trash, don't stash.** Keep a recycle bin near the entrance you most frequently use, so you can dispose of junk mail before it comes in the house. Next to the recycle bin, put a shredder to dispose of unwanted credit card offers and other junk mail immediately. In my home, the recycle bin and shredder sit side by side near the door in the garage. I pick up the mail and quickly review it for what can be immediately trashed or shredded. No junk mail darkens my doorstep.

- **File, don't pile.** In a convenient place near the door, set up a small file box and three folders:

  o *To do.* Place anything that needs action in this file folder, such as bills, invitations to RSVP, and forms to fill out.

  o *To file.* Slip receipts, bank statements, medical records—anything you need to keep—in this permanent or semi-permanent file.

  o *To read.* This folder is for magazines, newsletters—anything you'd like to read.

- **Urge to Purge.** Once a week, schedule thirty minutes to purge these files. Pay your bills. Respond to invitations. Transfer receipts and other paperwork to your permanent files. And finally, put your reading material in spots where you're likely to have snippets of time to read, such in your purse, by your tub, or on your bedside table.

So, you may be thinking, "What about the ten grocery sacks of paper in the hall closet that I haven't dealt with?" My advice: fuggedaboutit. At least for now. Concentrate on developing new habits, and then make plans to tackle that paper one sack at a time.

Cyndy

Diane
Sullivan

Storage Strategy

*Help! I've outgrown my home's storage even
though I have a storeroom filled with tons of
boxes. So much stuff and not enough space
in our home—can you give me some storage
tips?*

—Stuffed-Up Sue

Storage is a high priority for most people when they
choose a place to live. And any unused space can
quickly become a storeroom. Some storage areas are
full of containers nicely stacked and set in rows. Some
even *look* organized.

However, the contents of the containers may not
be relevant or useful in a person's life. It's like putting
a rug over a stain on the carpet: it looks good, but it's
disguising a mess.

The sad truth is, many people continue to buy more containers to store their stuff before they check the current containers to see what can be removed. Every so often, review what you have stored to see if you truly need to keep it. The result will be more usable space, and you'll be more organized.

Diane

Sheri
Lukasiewicz

Reaching Your Goal

I just don't get how people can be so different when it comes to organizing. What's your opinion?

—Wondering

Great question! And believe it or not, the answer is not as complicated as you might think. In fact, this dawned on me while I was doing something totally unrelated to organizing: standing outside with my son-in-law. He really likes cars, and couldn't help pointing out all the makes and models that tooled down the road into town. Some zipped by, while others seem to crawl down the road. But they all had one thing in common: they were heading toward their destination.

The same is true with organizing. There are many "makes" of people. Some are flashy in the way they do things; some are not. Some people zip along with stops and starts; others choose a slow and steady speed. The only thing that matters at the end of the day is whether they reach their goal. That's where the rubber meets the road.

Sheri

Donna
Schoeppner

Always Be Prepared

So many natural disasters are occurring around the world. How can I get my family prepared?

—Hoping not to blow away in Kansas

Take time to assemble the basic items that will make your life easier if your family is hit by a disaster. The Federal Emergency Management Agency (FEMA) recommends the following things for your disaster kit.

- Three-day supply of non-perishable food

- Three-day supply of water—one gallon of water per person per day

- Portable, battery-powered radio or television and extra batteries

- Flashlight and extra batteries

- First-aid kit and manual
- Sanitation and hygiene items (moist towelettes and toilet paper)
- Matches and waterproof container
- Whistle
- Extra clothing
- Kitchen accessories and cooking utensils, including a can opener
- Photocopies of credit and identification cards
- Cash and coins
- Special-needs items, such as prescription medications, eye glasses, contact lens solutions, and hearing aid batteries
- Items for infants, such as formula, diapers, bottles, and pacifiers
- Other items to meet your family's unique needs

Keep all items in a tightly closed plastic container, free from pests or other damage. Give some thought to where you store the container, making sure it will be handy if you have to stay in a safe place in your home or, heaven forbid, quickly evacuate.

Be sure to check the supplies every six months, swapping out the food and water. Schedule it on your calendar at the two times per year when severe weather is most likely to occur in your area.

Taking these few steps now could make a big difference to your family in the future.

Donna

Traci
Watkins

Little Things Add Up

I'm a single mom with three very active kids.
How can we stay organized?

—Overwhelmed in Omaha

I'll definitely take this question. As a single mom myself, I've found that little things can really make a difference in how a family functions. Here are my favorite timesavers that the kids can get involved with:

- **Create an organized departure.** Set up a landing pad for keys, wallet, phone, purse, and/or backpack. Use that spot to place anything that needs to go with you when you leave the house. It can also be a place to stick a reminder note for things you need to do. Put "ready-to-go" backpacks here or anything else you need to take (sports gear, dry cleaning, or an item to return to a store).

- **Keep cleaning supplies handy.** Cleaning is easier if your tools are conveniently located. Keep basic cleaning supplies in your kitchen and each bathroom. A caddy of dusting and other supplies would be handy on each floor of your home. You might even place a vacuum on each level.

- **Keep it close.** Keep a small basket near your couch or favorite chair for remote controls. Place spare items where you need them. For example, you may want extra reading glasses, a pen and paper, or lip balm in the family room. Keep a basket for magazines, letters, and catalogs near your reading chair.

These may seem like little things—but little things add up.

Traci

Jan
Limpach

A Fresh Look at Your Makeup

I can never pass up the cosmetic "gift with purchase." Consequently, I have drawers full of old makeup—some I've never used and would feel guilty just tossing in the trash.

—Made-Up in Manhattan

The first thing I have to tell you is to *let go of that guilt.* Old makeup is doing neither you nor anyone else a favor. Dermatologists warn that old foundation and sponges can harbor bacteria that cause of acne and blemishes. And if you value your eyesight, forget about hanging on to old mascara and eyeliner. Most eye makeup expires in just three months and may cause an eye infection if used after that date. Although cosmetics can be expensive, holding on to expired products has a higher price tag in regard to your health and safety.

Here are a few tips to give your makeup drawer a makeover:

- Toss out any makeup that has expired or that you're not using. Cosmetic experts say you should toss powders and eye shadows after two years, foundation and lipstick after one year, and mascara and eyeliner after three months. I recommend using a metallic silver or black marker to write the date of purchase on your cosmetics.

- Now that you've purged your cosmetics, it's time to organize and contain them. You might try a small caddy with a handle and dividers that can be easily stowed under the sink. You might even find one small enough to double for travel as well as for everyday use. A divided tray or basket can slip in a drawer or someplace out of sight. It just needs to be convenient and near where you use it.

For a fresh face, give your makeup drawer a fresh start!

Jan

Amy
Tokos

The Traveling Backpack

My bag overflows with my kids' stuff when we go on vacation. How can I lighten my load?

—Packing for Six

Traveling with a family is always an adventure. I have two words of advice for you: traveling backpack. Not yours—your kids'. Whether you're driving or flying, a traveling backpack for each of the kids is an easy way to keep all their stuff together—and out of your bag. I know you might be thinking, "Do you really mean only one backpack per child?" Yes, one backpack is all they need. Keep in mind that a child does not need entertainment for every minute of travel time. They are pretty resourceful and always seem to find ways to entertain themselves.

The two basic things to include in a child's traveling backpacks are fun and food.

- **Fun.** Have each child choose a few things to tuck in the backpack that will keep him or her entertained during the trip. Kids ages four and up can be responsible for picking their own toys (although feel free to make a few suggestions). Be careful about including toys with too many pieces. Self-sealing bags can also be great organizers. Your kids might want to make a list of what they put in their backpacks, so you don't leave anything behind.

- **Food.** Have the kids choose a few snacks to put in their backpacks. I like to give them a couple of snacks for morning and also slip some in my bag for the afternoon. This helps reduce non-stop snacking but also lets them have some control—taking me out of the food loop. I don't have to hear, "Mom, can I have..." or "Mom, will you pass the..." Sometimes, one of my kids will eat a snack before we leave the neighborhood, which is pretty funny.

If you're flying, it's important to make kids responsible for carrying their own backpacks. If you're driving, the backpack will keep a child from overpacking toys and reduces the clutter in the car.

Have fun and safe travels!

Amy

Suzette
Gavin

Organize the Bling

Diamonds may be a girl's best friend, but not being able to find my bling when I need it is a real problem. Any suggestions?

—Jewelry Junkie

When you can't find the necklace that goes with your little black dress or your bling gets buried in the bedroom, it's time to organize your jewelry.

- **Rings.** To organize rings, store them on a thread spool holder. You can find these where sewing supplies are sold.

- **Earrings.** If you have a large earring collection, you might store pairs in a mini-drawer unit that is meant for nuts and bolts. These are available at home improvement or discount department stores.

- **Necklaces and bracelets.** Cup hooks come in many different sizes and are great for hanging your necklaces and bracelets. Put them in your closet if you don't mind a few holes in the wall. Or consolidate the hooks on a thin paneling board, bulletin board, or foam board, and hang it in a convenient place. Another option for viewing all your necklace and bracelet choices is to install removable plastic hooks in your dressing area.

Finally, may you *always* have jewels to organize, my dear.

Suzette

Ellen
Hankes,
CPO-CD©

Letting Go of the Past—and the Stuff that Goes With It

I know you're an organizer and not a therapist. But I'd like to know why I can't get rid of anything. Do you have room on your couch to help me figure it out?

—Wondering

You're right—I'm not a therapist. But I do know from experience that people have their own reasons for why they hang on to certain items. For example, my dad was a great collector of hand-forged tools and unique agricultural items. Dad would often challenge us by asking, "Can you tell me how this tool was used?"

He encouraged us to look into the past and find relevance in the present and utility for the future.

Little did my dad know that he was helping to shape my philosophy as a professional organizer. When I work with clients, one of my primary jobs is to help them determine how much of their stuff is connected to the past, present, or future. For example, when going through a closet, a client might find a pair of jeans she hasn't worn for years. Understanding that this item is not relevant to her current situation makes it easier to release her to make space for a new pair of jeans.

So, do you have a hard time remembering why you've kept that kitchen gadget or pair of ill-fitting shoes all these years? If the reason is unclear, it may be time to think about passing the item on to someone who can use it in a meaningful way. On the other hand, with a little creativity you might be able to turn an item from your past into something you can use now or in the future. It's all about looking at the proportion of things you're keeping in terms of relevance to the past, present, and future. Make sure your possessions aren't keeping you mired in the past and preventing you from truly living in the present and preparing for the future.

Get up off the couch, my friend, and use those three mighty little words—past, present, future—to help you figure out why you're hanging on to certain items and to give you the freedom to let go.

Ellen

Jan
Limpach

Go the Extra Mile—
Recycle Your Pile

I'm passionate about recycling. I'm looking for more ways to satisfy my green side. Any ideas?

—Rickie in Rochester

I'm so pleased to hear you're passionate about recycling. Not too many people know that the average American family produces one hundred pounds of trash per week. Reducing what your family throws away by just 20 percent through recycling results in half a ton less going to a landfill each year. Sometimes it's hard being green, but, as you know, it's worth the effort.

Here are some ideas for incorporating recycling throughout your day: Start in the morning by recycling your cardboard cereal box, glass juice container, and plastic milk jug. Used coffee grounds make excellent mulch for acid-loving plants. There are also many items you can recycle after your shower. For example, when you open a new bar of soap, recycle the cardboard box. Don't forget the plastic bottles from the shampoo, conditioner, and shower gel.

Throughout the day, recycle newspapers, magazines, and junk mail. Don't forget to recycle the packaging from your meals and drinks from the day. You can even recycle empty tissue boxes and toilet paper rolls.

Daily life is full of opportunities to recycle. I like to tell people that they can change their mindsets from "Just throw it away!" to "What can I recycle today?" The reward is a cleaner, healthier world for our children and grandchildren.

Jan

Cyndy
Salzmann

Break the Procrastination Habit

I am a huge procrastinator. Help!

—Daisy Delay

There are lots of reasons for procrastinating, and some of them can be quite convincing. Trust me—my teenagers are masters at this. But even professional organizers understand that it's hard to make yourself do something that seems overwhelming, much less something you hate to do. So, here are some strategies to nudge you to the starting point:

- Break tasks into small steps. Yes, I know you've heard this before, but that's because it's so important. First make a list of the steps you need to take to reach your goal. Then tackle one step at a time, until you've finished the list.

- Start your day with a task that you tend to put off. Choose the thing you're most dreading to do and get it out of the way first thing in the morning. The rest of the day will be easier, and your mind will be free to focus on other things.

- Commit to spending just ten minutes a day working on a task you've been putting off. You'll be amazed how much you can get done in those few minutes, and it might give you the jump-start you need to cross it off your list.

It takes determination and effort to break the habit of procrastination. But when you do, you'll gain peace by eliminating the burden of a task left undone.

Cyndy

Diane
Sullivan

Organizing Dilemma

*My daughter and I share a bathroom, and
we have an ongoing conflict about the
placement of our beauty products. I like things
all lined up, She just puts items where they are
the easiest to get to. Who's right?*

—Minneapolis Mom

Sometimes being organized doesn't look organized. I
recently solved a similar dilemma with my bathroom
shelves. I had everything lined up, with short items in
the front and tall in the back. It looked so neat and
organized. While it looked beautiful, it just didn't work
for me.

You see, my hairspray was in the back of the shelf
because it was tall. Each time I used it, I knocked over
everything else trying to put it back. I fought that battle
many times before I came up with the brilliant solution

of moving that tall can of hair spray to the front. It doesn't look as nice, but it sure is a lot handier. And that's what being organized is all about.

One of the key principles of organizing is to place items you use the most, front and center. While this doesn't always look the best, it will serve you well in the long run. Kudos to your daughter; she may be on her way to becoming a professional organizer.

Diane

Suzette
Gavin

Catch It in the Closet

I have three kids, and when we come in the door the mittens and scarves fly. They never make it to the closet. Any tips?

—Out of the Closet

Unfortunately hall closets just don't have enough space for all the gear they need to hold. Entry or rear-door closets at best have a hanging rod and a shelf that no one can reach. Here are a few tips for catching family outerwear and more in the hall closet:

- **Hats, gloves, and scarves**. Depending on the number of people in your household, use a clear plastic box (about the size of two shoe boxes placed side by side) for these items. Place it where all members of the family can get to it easily. Labels like "Snow Gear" and

"Mom's Scarves" will help you remember what goes where.

- **Small stuff**. To make it easy for three children to put away their own items, purchase a three-drawer unit (about the size of a small chest of drawers). Put it in your closet, or, if it's attractive, even in your entryway. All the small stuff—gloves, mittens, hats, and scarves—can go there. If you have more hanging space than floor space, use a hanging storage unit to give each child a cubby to corral mittens and stocking caps.

- **Umbrellas**. Hang a coat hook just inside the door on both sides of your coat closet. These are great for umbrellas as well as ball caps and reusable shopping bags.

If you make storage easy and accessible for children, their stuff is less likely to land on the floor. Go beyond the shelf and rod, and catch those flying mittens in the closet.

Suzette

Donna
Schoeppner

Six Slick Tips to Keep You Organized

I feel I'm fairly organized, but would love some time- and money-saving tips. Any ideas?

—Almost There

Try these easy tips to keep you headed in the right direction:

1. Every time you leave a room, pick up something that doesn't belong in that space. This will help you get into the habit of returning things to their homes.

2. If you can do something in two minutes or less, do it *now*.

3. If you're looking for a time to read, keep a magazine or book in your car. If you get caught in traffic or are waiting to pick up the kids, this is a great opportunity to catch up on your reading.

4. When you remove an article of clothing from your closet, move the empty hanger to a designated spot. It might be at the end of a rod, on a hook, or in a basket. Creating a home for hangers makes laundry day a breeze.

5. Use a lingerie bag to simplify the laundry process. Each person in the house can place his or her dirty undergarments and socks into the mesh bag. The bag goes into the washer, then the dryer, and then to the person's room. This means less sorting and hopefully less loss to the Land of Lost Socks.

6. When traveling by air, slide a collapsible bag into the side pocket of your suitcase. If you acquire souvenirs along the way, the extra bag will provide a way to get them home. On several vacations, this extra bag saved me money. I avoided paying an overweight bag charge or extra bag fee.

These ideas should keep you moving toward your quest to be even more organized.

Donna

Traci
Watkins

Mind over Clutter

I'm not an organized person. I try, but my home is still a mess. Help?

—Desperate in Denver

Sometimes a disordered space can be more about what's cluttering your mind than what's cluttering your home. Negative thoughts can sabotage your efforts and keep you from even starting an organizing project. I refer to this as "mind clutter," and it can be just as daunting as the piles on your countertop.

Here are three tips to help you break through the mental mess:

- **Visualize *your goal and put it in writing.*** A great way to motivate yourself to get started on an organizing project is to visualize the result. Picture how the space will work, look, and make you feel. Then write down your vision by completing a sentence such as, "Now that ____ is organized, I can _____." For example, "Now that my kitchen is organized, I can have my neighbors over for dinner." You might even post this statement in a prominent place or say it out loud.

- **Believe *you can achieve your vision by setting realistic goals.*** Now take your vision to the next level by truly believing it's possible. Belief in yourself is a powerful motivator. You'll also gain confidence when you break down a goal into small, manageable steps. For example, a step toward an organized kitchen might be to clear the table each day.

- **Overcome *obstacles with gratitude and affirmation.*** Everyone gets stuck. When you start to feel your motivation slipping away, use an affirmation such as, "I love that I can keep my counters clean." Also, be thankful for each small step such as, "I'm so grateful that I can watch my kids do their homework at the kitchen table while I cook dinner." This type of positive self-talk will help you move ahead.

Bottom line: Don't let mind clutter hold you back. Cast a vision, make a plan, and think positively.

Traci

Ashley
Kates

Just Ten More Minutes

The alarm rings way too early most mornings, and yet we never seem to make it out the door in time. What ideas do you have for a morning makeover?

—Bedhead

If you're like me in the morning, you're praying for just ten more minutes of sleep. Do you feel disorganized and rushed getting out the door the moment your feet hit the floor? Here's the secret: preparing the night before contributes to a successful morning exit.

- **Assemble lunches.** Keep or make snack size containers of lunch foods such as carrots and crackers on hand. Most lunches can be made and refrigerated the night before so they are handy the next morning. Make sure the lunches are labeled so Dad doesn't grab the kiddo's peanut-butter-and-jelly sandwich and drink box.

- **Select clothing.** Each family member can lay out clothes in the evening, complete with accessories, socks, and underwear.

- **Check schedules for activities.** Collect the music books, sports equipment, or library books. Be sure the necessary items are in the appropriate bags to eliminate last-minute dashes.

- **Create and use a launch pad by the door.** Put the backpacks, gym bags, and purses in a group near the door, easily accessible for the walk out.

It's all about preparation. Just a few minutes of thought and preparation the night before can give you a few more minutes in the morning to start the day off right.

Ashley

Amy
Tokos

No Shopping Required

My collection of organizing books is extensive, and I'm the first in line for the latest and greatest organizing product. Why do I still feel hopelessly unorganized?

—*Lost in the Aisles*

There are a few things that we tend to do when we are trying to get organized. We buy products that promise to solve our organization challenges, and we purchase books that promise an organized life. Then, when "it" doesn't work, we feel discouraged and hopelessly unorganized.

Products and books can be helpful, but there really should be an asterisk by their descriptions. Here's what I have in mind:

Organizing Product A*

*To know if this product will work for you, clean out your clutter before purchase. Do not purchase this item until you have done the work. Look around to see if you already have something in your home that can give you the same result as this product. It's better for the environment and pocketbook if you can recycle or reuse an item you already have.

Organizing Book*

*Every home and person is different, so every solution in this book may not work for you. If you have a system that's working, don't make changes just because this book suggests certain procedures. Find things you like in this book and try them, adjusting them to work with your lifestyle.

Marketers would never put these statements on their products, but you can do it for yourself. Admittedly, there are some great organizing products and books out there. On the other hand, any professional organizer will tell you that the products and books don't hold the real secret to getting organized. The real secret is to minimize the stuff.

Nobody is hopelessly unorganized. You just have to figure out what works best for you.

Amy

Sheri
Lukasiewicz

Getting from To-Do to Ta-Da!

I'm great at making to-do lists, but at end of the day nothing is crossed off. How do I get from my long list to "Ta da, I'm done"?

—Good at Lists

You can transform your to-do list into a helpful ally that keeps you moving toward the next task. Your evil nemesis, the list, reminds you of your failures and shortcomings. But you can make peace with your to-do list.

I don't want to get preachy about how you make your list. Do what works for you. It can be on a slip of paper, a spreadsheet, your phone, or whatever is convenient for you.

Here are a few tips for using your list:

- When you're compiling your list, just write things as they come to you. Don't worry about putting them in order of importance. After you've made your list, number your priorities but don't overcomplicate that either. Don't spend a lot of time mulling over which should be first and which should be second. If two tasks are high priorities, work to get them both done on target. For example, paying the utility bill and taking your child to a dentist appointment will both be important tasks for the day. Which is first and which is second isn't worth a lot of deep thought. While dusting may be on your list, perhaps it can wait. After all, the dust will still be there tomorrow.

- Devote an area at the bottom of your list for tasks that you'd like to get done at some point. They can come under your SDS (Some Day Soon) category. These tasks may include sorting through pictures or organizing recipes. Use this part of the list as a long-term reminder.

- Check items off when you've done them. Do you get great satisfaction from checking things off your list? I do! In fact, I often write things down that aren't on my list after I do them, just so I can have the satisfaction of seeing those big, fat checkmarks. I know it may sound crazy, but it feels good.

Remember, you're master of the list, not the other way around. Make it your ally. Identify and complete priority items, and carry over your SDS to another day. At the end of the day, you'll shout "Ta da!"

Sheri

Authors

Suzette Gavin
An Organized Life
www.anorganizedlifeplan.com

Suzette Gavin began creating checklists in her teens, due to the activities in which she was involved. She started extensive work with filing systems and office organization when working as a property manager for local, regional, and large national property management companies. Her office experience grew with each promotion as she worked her way from leasing agent at a large residential complex to managing a portfolio of fifteen shopping centers.

When moving to different locations within the U.S. for new job opportunities, she gained a great deal of knowledge of not only how to organize a move to a new location but also how to set up a new residence. It was a natural fit for her to become a professional organizer. Her company, An Organized Life, was founded in March 2005.

Suzette continues to love her career choice as a professional organizer, and the satisfying rewards it offers by helping those in need. On the fun side of life, she enjoys music, whether it's playing the piano or dancing. She cannot deny her "happy feet" when a good song comes on the radio. She also adores her two cats as they sit in the middle of her desk when she is trying to work.

Ellen Hankes CPO-CD©
Calahan Solutions Inc.
www.calahansolutions.com

Ellen believes each person is unique and has a special set of organizing needs. When clutter and chaos keep you from meeting your goals, that's when Ellen steps in to help. Her skills and experience help those on the more extreme end of the disorganization spectrum. As a Certified Professional Organizer in Chronic Disorganization, she specializes in working with individuals and families affected by chronic disorganization and hoarding behaviors. Ellen is always up for an adventure—near or far. Walking with her husband of forty years and giggling with her grandson and granddaughter are two of her favorite pastimes.

Ashley Kates
Life Contained
www.lifecontained.net

Ashley reminds us to be inspired to let organization enter our life and be motivated by the changes of new systems and functionality. She finds her energetic personality, patience, and unique perspective motivates people to embrace organizational change.

When Ashley's not organizing, you may find her occupied with photography, dancing, cooking with her husband, kickboxing, traveling, scouting out a new adventure or hobby, or spending time with family and friends.

Jan Limpach
Organizing Plus®
www.OrganizingPlus.com

Jan has been a professional organizer for over twenty years and loves working with people to help them "find what they need, when they need it." She organizes homes, offices, and moves, helping people stay on track when they are ready to change their lives.

Jan is a nationally known speaker and an avid writer who has been featured in national publications, including the *New York Times*, *Wall Street Journal*, *Better Homes and Gardens*, and *Good Housekeeping*. She has been happily married for forty years, and having kids and grandkids is the highlight of her life. She knows that having a busy family means you have to be organized to run a household smoothly. She enjoys life to the fullest, and some of her biggest blessings call her Grandma.

Sheri Lukasiewicz
Peace by Piece
www.pbyponline.com

Professional organizer and finance coach Sheri Lukasiewicz is excited to bring organization to your home and business spaces, knowing the peace and productivity it brings. She is able to assist you not only with your office, craft room, closets, and pantry, but also with your computer files and bill-paying technique.

Sheri is passionate about helping others who feel overwhelmed by debt. She completed Dave Ramsey Financial Counselor training and loves to coach others to financial freedom through his common-sense, proven methods. Sheri very recently entered a fun season of her life when she became a member of grandmotherhood.

Cyndy Salzmann
America's Clutter Coach™
www.cyndysalzmann.com

Affectionately known as America's Clutter Coach™, Cyndy is a multi-published author and popular national speaker. One of her most popular topics is the organizing philosophy she developed, based on both research and experience. Organized by Design begins with a personality test to help both audiences and individual clients discover their unique organizing styles. This assessment is the basis for identifying organizational systems that build on personal strengths for lasting improvement.

Donna Schoeppner
Schoeppner Organizing Solutions
www.SchoeppnerOrganizingSolutions.com

Donna's organizing motto is "Simplify Your Space. Simplify Your Life." Helping her clients find solutions to create and maintain a simpler, less complicated life is her passion. She also enjoys learning her clients' life stories. Donna loves spending time with family and friends. She is game for just about any new adventure, from snorkeling to skydiving.

Diane Sullivan
The Organization Station
www.organization-station.net

Diane is all about the *fun* in life. She believes being more organized allows more free time to enjoy all that life has to offer, especially with family and friends. She knows the challenges derived from an overwhelming workload, "stuff" issues and the many decisions you face every day. Saving you time is her specialty.

Diane is the author of an organizing book titled *Myth or Reality? Weekends FREE!* She is the recipient of the National Association of Professional Women (NAPW) Women of the Year award. Diane loves to be involved, whether in civic and community causes or in planning social events.

Amy Tokos
Freshly Organized
www.freshlyorganized.com

Keep it simple. These words describe Amy's organizing philosophy. Having the opportunity to help others make their home more organized and enjoyable is why she likes being a professional organizer. With four active kids of her own, she knows the daily challenges of keeping a family organized and finding balance.

You may wonder if Amy's house is in perfect order. Well, it isn't. Her home is what she calls "organized chaos." Her training as an engineer helps to keep it organized, and her children help make it a bit chaotic. She says the key is to keep expectations realistic and honor your priorities. This definitely helps to keep things "real" at the Tokos house.

Traci Watkins
Professional Reliable Organizing
www.prorganzing.com

Traci wants to help you overcome obstacles that are keeping you from enjoying your life or your spaces. Her goal is to create organizing and time-management systems that are tailored to your work style so that they can easily be maintained long-term. Traci is a single mom who has a passion for efficiency so she can spend more time with her son and her dog, and enjoy the other great things in life.°

Index

21698502R00109

Made in the USA
Lexington, KY
24 March 2013